Understanding the Sacred

Understanding the Sacred

Sociological Theology for Contemporary People

Murray Milner Jr.

WIPF & STOCK · Eugene, Oregon

UNDERSTANDING THE SACRED
Sociological Theology for Contemporary People

Copyright © 2019 Murray Milner Jr. All rights reserved. Except for brief quotations in critical publications or reviews, no part of this book may be reproduced in any manner without prior written permission from the publisher. Write: Permissions, Wipf and Stock Publishers, 199 W. 8th Ave., Suite 3, Eugene, OR 97401.

Wipf & Stock
An Imprint of Wipf and Stock Publishers
199 W. 8th Ave., Suite 3
Eugene, OR 97401

www.wipfandstock.com

PAPERBACK ISBN: 978-1-5326-6640-7
HARDCOVER ISBN: 978-1-5326-6641-4
EBOOK ISBN: 978-1-5326-6642-1

Scripture quotations are taken from the New Revised Standard Version (NRSV), copyright ©1989 by the Division of Christian Education of the National Council of Churches of Christ in the U.S.A. Used with permission. All rights reserved.

Manufactured in the U.S.A.

For the members of the Contemporary Theology class Westminster Presbyterian Church, Charlottesville, Virginia, 2015–2018

Other books by Murray Milner Jr.

Freaks, Geeks, and Cool Kids: Teenagers in an Era of Consumerism, Standardized Tests, and Social Media, revised edition (Routledge 2015)

Elites: A General Model (Polity 2014)

Freaks, Geeks, and Cool Kids: American Teenagers, Schools, and the Culture of Consumption (Routledge 2004)

Status and Sacredness: A General Theory of Status Relations and an Analysis of Indian Culture (Oxford University Press 1994)

Unequal Care: A Case Study of Interorganizational Relations in Health Care (Columbia University Press 1980)

The Illusion of Equality: The Effects of Education on Opportunity, Inequality, and Social Conflict (Jossey-Bass 1972)

Police on Campus: The Mass Police Action at Columbia University, Spring 1968 (New York Civil Liberties Union 1969); with others

The word must become flesh, but the flesh also must become word. It is not enough for us, as human beings, just to live. We also must give words to what we are living.

—HENRI J. M. NOUWEN[1]

---

1. Nouwen, *Bread for the Journey*, June 24.

Contents

Preface | xi

Chapter 1: Introduction: The Problem | 1
Chapter 2: Religion, Sacredness, and Status | 11
Chapter 3: Meaning, Mystery, Magic, Metaphor, and Explanation | 17
Chapter 4: Some Classical Doctrines in a New Language | 33
Chapter 5: The Church | 51
Chapter 6: More Doctrines in a New Language | 63
Chapter 7: Worship | 83
Chapter 8: Is There a God? | 95
Chapter 9: Conclusion | 106

Appendix: Discussion Questions | 111
Bibliography | 115
Index | 119

Preface

HUMANS HAVE LONG STRUGGLED to make sense of their lives—and their deaths. They also ponder the source and nature of existence itself. Creation stories from many cultures attest to this.

Most people seek to find meaning by placing their personal and local experiences in the context of some broader story. Historically such stories have usually been remembered and passed on by an extended set of social relationships, that is, by a religious institution. Christians call this institution the church. The church includes those who have studied and reflected upon these stories and related religious experiences. They are called theologians and their reflections are theology.

The job of theologians is to create doctrines: ideas about a particular part of religious experiences; for example, how we praise God. Such doctrines are not only informational, they also evaluate. In praising God, singing hymns is appropriate; sacrificing children is not.

Most Christian doctrines were formulated centuries ago. Often, they involve notions that are hard for contemporary people to accept: for example, belief in a virgin birth or that the Bible is the literal word of God dictated to some human scribe.

What this book does is focus on the concerns behind the classical doctrines of Christianity. Then it provides new ways of thinking and talking about these doctrines. I do not claim that the new suggested images and concepts are the only appropriate way to think about these doctrines. Those who find traditional doctrines meaningful should be respected—as long as they respect others.

This means all theology should avoid demeaning women, people of color, those from different cultural backgrounds—and those who call into question the adequacy of the traditional doctrines. On the other hand, this does not mean anything goes; civil critique and debate should be encouraged.

But the rapid decline in church membership shows that for contemporary people in the West, traditional doctrines are inadequate. Meaningful doctrines are not the core of the church's religious life—but they are essential. This book is a contribution to reformulating this crucial element of church life in language and images most people can understand.

Chapter 1

Introduction: The Problem

Need for a New Language

ABOUT TWO YEARS AGO I ran into an old friend. She had long been a very active member of my church, but for some months she had not been coming. When I asked her why, she said, "I just can't keep saying things I don't really believe." She represents an increasing number of people—including the teenagers and adult children of many faithful church members. The traditional concepts of theology are increasingly alien to many members and potential members of the church.

How many educated people really believe in any literal sense the following words of the Apostle's Creed: "conceived by the Holy Spirit, born of the Virgin Mary . . . was crucified, died . . . and on the third day he rose again"? When they say the Nicene Creed, how many understand the significance of "begotten, not made, being of one substance with the Father"?[1] Even relatively recent creeds by progressive denominations use such language as: "God raised this Jesus from the dead, vindicating his sinless life, breaking the power of sin and evil, delivering us from death to life eternal."[2] How many contemporary people find this creditable?

---

1. If the Father "made" the Son, that would suggest that there was a time when the Son did not exist and that at a later time he was made by the Father. "Begotten" is intended to finesse this issue and affirm that the Son (and the Holy Spirit) have always existed in fellowship with the Father and that the three form the triune God. Unsurprisingly this issue has long been discussed by theologians.

2. Presbyterian Church (U.S.A), "Brief Statement of Faith."

1

Such phrases may be familiar and even comforting. But will such language articulate the Christian faith in a way that will appeal to contemporary people, especially those who have not been brought up in the church—which is now a majority of the population in the U.S. and Europe? In the future, such traditional theological language is even less likely to be meaningful to educated people—and the education level of people in the U.S. and Europe is steadily increasing.

An aside is required. Of course, some highly educated people still affirm traditional doctrines and creeds, but generally there is a negative correlation between education and religious belief and participation. In the context of Western societies, when I refer to "educated people" I mean those with "some college" or more.

Reducing racial, gender, and income inequality, demoting patriarchal images, assisting refugees, and welcoming LGBTs are important steps toward justice and inclusivity. These do not, however, address a more fundamental theological issue: articulating ideas that are believable and meaningful to people in modern and postmodern societies. In an age of democratic republics, are images of God as "Lord," "King," and "Master" compelling? Are people able and willing to think of themselves as "slaves," "servants," and "subjects"? In a world where very few people have had any direct experience with agriculture, will images of sheep, shepherds, sowers, and harvesting capture their existential experiences? Will people in the future commit to a religious faith in which the key images and concepts fail to reflect any of their actual experiences—or the experiences of anyone they know? Another way of asking this question is: would the biblical faith have sustained itself, much less spread, if it had drawn primarily on images from hunting and gathering societies?

The implication of these observations is not that we should abandon biblical images or all of the traditional religious concepts. Abandoning the past completely is virtually impossible. None of us gives up our mother tongue and creates a totally new language. Language—like religion—is always a collective project linked to a

INTRODUCTION: THE PROBLEM

past.[3] We can, however, become "multilingual" and ecumenical. We need to be conversant in languages of both the past and the present, of both the mundane empirical world and the transcendent symbolic world. Some languages eventually become a "dead language." Some religious doctrines will gradually fade away and become historical relics.

Academic disciplines often rely on meta-languages, that is, they draw on specialized languages as a means of talking about the problems that concern them. For example, physics relies heavily on mathematics. Traditionally, theology has primarily used philosophy as a meta-language. Theologians have drawn on a wide array of philosophies to articulate their understandings. Augustine (354-430 AD) utilized Neoplatonism, Aquinas (1225-1274 AD) used Aristotle, Paul Tillich (1886-1965) drew on Platonism and existentialism, and process theology employed Alfred North Whitehead's (1861-1947) philosophy.[4] Some contemporary theology has used other meta-languages; for example, narrative theology has drawn on literary theory. If the criteria of success is the revitalization of North American and European churches, these philosophical and literary efforts have largely failed. They have not developed new concepts and notions that the typical minister or person-in-the-pew find comprehensible and meaningful—and have incorporated in the liturgy and prayers.

By profession, I am a sociologist. Much of my research and writing has focused on how status systems work. (Status is the accumulated expressions of approval and disapproval directed toward an object, actor, activity, or category. More on this later.) My work has included analyses of the Indian caste system, American teenagers, Indian teenagers, celebrities, human rights, elites, and religion.

---

3. Even deliberately created languages such as Esperanto have drawn on previous languages.

4. I am aware that most scholars of religion use BCE (Before the Common Era) and CE (Common Era) rather than the more traditional BC (Before Christ) and AD (Anno Domini ("in the year of the Lord"). It is my impression, however, that the new usage is not well-known beyond the scholarly community. Hence, my use of the traditional labels is primarily to aid in communication rather than to attribute theological value to the older terms.

3

Much of religious activity has to do with how people relate to what they consider sacred. A useful way to think of sacredness is to see it as the highest and ultimate form of status, the thing we value most. Consequently, this book focuses on how the concepts of status and sacredness (and other sociological concepts) are useful in outlining a new way to think and talk about religious experience—in a language that makes sense to contemporary people.

People have at least an intuitive sense of how status systems operate, which helps to make a sociological theology more accessible and meaningful. This book is an attempt by a Christian who is a sociologist to articulate a theology for laity, clergy, and theologians who find much of the traditional religious language problematic.

What Is Theology?

As I will use the word, it refers to the attempt of people to explain the content of their religious beliefs and practices. It draws primarily on *language*, including the use of specialized concepts. (This is in contrast to other legitimate forms of religious expression, such as visual images, music, meditation techniques, or bodily movements.) Systematic theology focuses especially on the doctrines of a religious group.[5] Both "theology" and "doctrine" have become "dirty words." Often people assume these involve rigidity, denial, intolerance. Theology need not deny what science has taught us, and doctrine need not be dogmatic. Theology and doctrine should seek clarity, using language and concepts that are generally familiar to those concerned. While ambiguity and even paradox can be legitimate in some forms of religious expression, they should be used sparingly in systematic theology. This does not mean that

---

5. This is in contrast the Sarah Coakley's project of *theology totale*, which attempts to collapse the boundaries between articulating doctrines using words with ritual and other non-verbal forms of communication. Both approaches are legitimate but if the first volume of her proposed four volume systematic theology is any indicator, broadening the scope of theology will only make it more complex and difficult for laity and clergy to grasp.

INTRODUCTION: THE PROBLEM

theology can or should be restricted to literal description and logically derived propositions. Often it will draw on metaphors and other less literal figures of speech.

In some respects, theology is paradoxical; it attempts to be clear about what is inherently a mystery. A core characteristic of the holy and the sacred is its otherness, its difference from the ordinary.[6] Otherness makes it unfamiliar, mysterious, and unknowable. However, recognizing the inevitability of mystery does not mean that one must engage in magic and mystification. *Affirming mystery and the limits of human knowledge should not be an excuse for ignoring and denying what we do know about the empirical world.*

Historically, theologians have developed two ways of dealing with the mysterious otherness of God. A long tradition of "negative" theology says we can only say what God is not. An equally long "positive" tradition, while recognizing the limits of what we can know, insists that it is crucial that religious people articulate what they believe. (Theologians often refer to the negative approach as *apophatic* theology, while the positive approach is called *cataphatic* theology). Both negative and positive approaches recognize that theology and doctrine is certainly not the only, or even the most important, kind of religious activity. Much of religious life is *not* primarily about communicating our faith in words and concepts. Worship, pastoral care, building and organizational maintenance, helping the needy, and seeking social justice are also essential elements of most religious traditions and especially of Christians influenced by Jesus's teachings and life.

Granted that theology and doctrine are not the core of religious life, nonetheless they play a legitimate and essential role in defining membership and acceptable behavior within a particular religious group. Theology as I define it is the "head-trip" part of religion, more a matter of careful thinking than emotion. Another way of saying this is that both our beliefs and our emotions are central to a fruitful religious life. However, it is hard to commit one's heart to churches that want us to believe the unbelievable.

---

6. See Otto, *The Idea of the Holy*, for the classic discussion of the holy.

UNDERSTANDING THE SACRED

Individuals and groups vary on whether they emphasize the head or the heart, but to neglect either is a mistake. This is not a "devotional" or "inspirational" book in the usual sense of these words. Yet it is concerned about devotion and inspiration. My strategy is to facilitate devotion and inspiration by lessening the gap between traditional religious language and what people find both credible and inspiring.

Virtually all social groups have "doctrines." These can come in a variety of forms: taken-for-granted conventions, kinship rules, statements of purpose, constitutions, bylaws, and organizational charts are some examples. Some doctrines deal with *the assumed state of the world*. The American Declaration of Independence expresses a set of doctrines: "We hold these truths to be self-evident, that all men are created equal, that they are endowed by their Creator with certain unalienable Rights that among these are Life, Liberty and the pursuit of Happiness." The Bible makes statements not only about humans and their finitude—"and to dust you shall return" (Genesis 3:19)—but about the value of the creation—"and indeed it was very good" (Genesis 1:31). Other doctrines are ideologies in the sense that they indicate the way things are supposed to be: "You shall have no other gods before me" (Exodus 20:3).[7] The doctrine of equality before the law—that is, providing everyone with the same due process—is an ideal, but seldom a reality. Groups vary widely in how explicitly and rigorously their doctrinal criteria are stated and enforced. That is, groups vary in how doctrinaire their doctrine is. Groups with no doctrine and no functioning boundaries can seldom sustain themselves. If a housing co-op does not distinguish between members and non-members, it is likely to be filled with people who have not contributed to buying and maintaining the property. Boundaries can also be too rigid. Highly rigid and demanding doctrine typically leads to schisms, whether in religious groups, political parties, or intellectual and artistic movements.[8]

---

7. For a discussion of how I use the word "ideology" see my *Elites: A General Model*, 35–36. The word is used in a number of different senses and the most that I can do is be clear about how I am using the concept.

8. A couple of examples: Since very conservative leaders took control of

INTRODUCTION: THE PROBLEM

Both conservative Baptist and radical Marxist political parties tend to have numerous disagreements and splits. Social groups, including religious communities, vary in how they handle disagreements about the content and meaning of doctrine. For the U.S. legal system, a series of appeals courts decide what is to be the correct interpretation of legal doctrines. For the Roman Catholic Church, the pope has the final decision about what doctrines mean and how the rules are to be enforced. Most Reformed churches (e.g., Presbyterians) have a series of assemblies of clergy and laity (e.g., presbyteries, synods, general assemblies) that make final decisions about doctrines and rules. Other non-religious civic groups also have some structure and procedures for settling disagreements.

While theology and doctrine are not the central part of religious life, *they are essential*. Moreover, it is important that religious people have some sense of what these guiding ideas are—and that these official ideas are intelligible and meaningful to most of the group's members. For many contemporary Christians these requirements seem increasingly problematic. Theology is a reflection upon what religious people believe and do—and vice versa. The religion that cannot articulate a convincing theology is not likely to sustain itself in the contemporary world, especially in societies with high levels of education.

But what about God? The word "theology" has two roots: *theo* (i.e., about God) + *ology* (the study of). Consequently, whether or not God exists is a crucial issue. What is the point in talking about theology if there is no God? I agree that the issue must be addressed. The doctrine of God is not, however, the best place to

---

the Southern Baptist Convention in the 1980s, several state conventions (e.g. Virginia and Texas) have withdrawn support from the national convention, and major Baptist universities (e.g. Wake Forest and Baylor) have become independent rather than denominational institutions. While the number of avowed Communists in the U.S. has always been a small percentage of the population, they have repeatedly split into multiple parties—often over disagreements about how to interpret Marx and Lenin or how closely to adhere to the ideology and policies of either the Soviet Union or Maoist China.

begin. Hence, I would ask the skeptic to be patient; I will address this question toward the end of this very short book.

Theology for Whom?

Theology is written from a particular perspective for a particular audience. I want to make clear the perspective from which I write and who may find my ideas most useful. I grew up in a central Texas town of about fifteen thousand people that was generally conservative: theologically, socially, and politically. Nonetheless, since high school I have been a member of relatively liberal Protestant churches. After college, I attended Union Theological Seminary in New York City and Columbia University. I became a professional sociologist. I first taught at New York University (NYU), but I have spent most of my career at the University of Virginia (UVA). I have lived in the UK three times and in South Asia four times—either running a relief and development program, teaching, or doing research. As indicated above, much of my scholarly work has focused on status systems, and I will draw on these ideas and other sociological concepts to suggest a new approach to theology.

While I hope to influence how scholars think about religion and theology, I have minimized summarizing the work of modern theologians—even renowned ones such as Karl Barth, Emil Brunner, Paul Tillich, Charles Hartshorne, Rosemary Radford Reuther, Jurgen Moltmann, and Sarah Coakley. That would require a very different kind of book.

What I have to say is aimed especially at those who are skeptical of much of the traditional formulations of Christian theology. Obviously, scholars who are atheist or agnostics fall into this category, but so do many religiously committed scholars.

I especially try to speak to many church members who find it harder and harder to think about their faith in literal understandings of the Bible and the language of traditional creeds. Often, they find fellowship and support in their local congregations but in effect tune out or cross their fingers when they are asked to recite or

INTRODUCTION: THE PROBLEM

affirm traditional creeds. I hope that my readers will also include clergy who are pastors to such people.

A third intended audience is those whom I will call "seekers." These are people with little or no connection with Christian churches but who have a sense that contemporary secular culture is inadequate and perhaps ultimately vacuous—in part because of its preoccupation with economic growth and consumption. They often express this by saying that they are "spiritual but not religious." Many of these are my academic colleagues. Others are knowledgeable, thoughtful, and caring people seeking something that transcends the pursuit of "more stuff," "more choices," or "moving up." Some combination of scholars, church members (and their clergy), and seekers are my wished-for audience.

The abandonment of religion in general and the decline of traditional or "mainline" churches in the U.S. and Europe is my concern. ("Mainline" is primarily an American term that refers to well-established denominations as contrasted to relatively new "evangelical" or "megachurches." In many European countries, there is a similar differentiation though different terms are used.) As a recent study by the Pew Foundation makes clear, the number and percentage of Americans who say they are religious has been steadily declining—especially among young people. Those who said they are religiously "unaffiliated" went from 16 percent in 2007 to 23 percent in 2014, and recent research indicates that is very likely to continue.[9] This trend is even more common in Europe, where a relatively small minority regularly attends church. The portion of people in England and Wales who identify as Christian fell from 71.7 percent in 2001 to 59.3 percent in 2011, and those reporting no religion increased from 14.8 percent to 25.1 percent.[10] A 2010 European Commission poll reported that in France 54 percent of the population "tend not to trust" religious institutions while this figure was 62 percent in Belgium, 50 percent in Germany, and 47 percent in the UK. In short, there has clearly been an erosion of

---

9. See, for example, Lipka, *Changing U.S Religious Landscape*, and Brauer, "Surprising Predictable Decline."

10. Office of National Statistics (UK), *Religion in England and Wales*.

9

religious commitment across most of Europe and the U.S., and this is especially the case among Christians.[11]

In Africa, Asia, and Latin American the Christian church is experiencing significant revitalization and growth—generally among people with relatively low levels of wealth and education. They are drawn primarily to liberation theology and Pentecostalism—and they may well be the core of the future church. Jesus' preference for the poor is (and should be) a key element of Christianity. Black theology takes into account the discrimination that Blacks have experienced; it also attempts to minister to Black churches and encourages these churches to develop forms of power that can end discrimination. The varied and extensive developments of feminist theology speak to women, but also call the church and the culture to take seriously both discrimination against women and their crucial contribution to the life and history of Christianity. The need for theologies that consider the particular experiences of disadvantaged groups is not, however, a legitimate excuse to give up on others; God loves the privileged as well as the underprivileged. We need theologies that speak to all of these groups and that help to reduce the material and spiritual distance between them. As a relatively privileged White male, I am not the one to attempt to articulate the experiences and particular needs of disadvantaged groups. While drawing on these traditions, I suspect that what I have to say will most appeal to relatively educated members of the middle class.

Now we must turn to the task of clarifying the nature of religion, sacredness, and status.

---

11. European Commission, *Public Opinion*.

Chapter 2

Religion, Sacredness, and Status

What Is Religion?

SCHOLARS HAVE LONG DEBATED how to define religion and related concepts.[1] This is an especially complicated issue for those wanting to look at religion across different societies and time periods. But my concern here is not to solve the problems of comparative religion, but to provide a vocabulary that will be meaningful to educated contemporary Christians. I will draw on a number of related concepts, for example, religious, secular, sacred, profane, transcendent, and mundane. I will not, however, attempt to provide a systematic discussion of these concepts—that would require a different book.

In addition to definitions there is the issue of boundaries. In simple societies with low levels of social differentiation, it can be difficult to distinguish religion from other activities. More complex societies usually have identifiable specialized social institutions devoted to particular concerns, but clear boundaries delineating each of these types of activities are rare. The boundaries of what is political, economic, educational, artistic, or religious are at best fuzzy. I am not saying that these distinctions are not useful, but only that trying to set unambiguous boundaries is probably a fool's errand.

For reasons that will become apparent in the rest of the book I will focus primarily on the notion of sacredness. This follows

---

1. See for example, Casanova, "Private and Public Religion"; Smith, *Meaning and End of Religion*; and Dubuisson, *Theory in Religion*, 26–30.

11

UNDERSTANDING THE SACRED

French sociologist Emile Durkheim (1858–1917), who argued that central to most religious activity is some distinction between what is *sacred* and what is *profane*.[2] Sacred objects, actors, activities, and categories are usually treated with some combination of fear, deference, respect, reverence, admiration, esteem, and veneration—at least by those who consider them sacred. A location or object may be considered sacred, but they are not usually considered acting subjects.[3] Gods are sacred, but they have the additional characteristics of subjectivity and intentionality. So, if a useful way to define religion is to focus on what is sacred, this raises the question of how we can better understand the source and nature of sacredness.

One useful way to think of *sacredness* is to consider it as *the highest form of status*. An advantage of thinking of the sacred as a particular form of status is that most of us are familiar with status and status systems: in our jobs, neighborhoods, schools, and voluntary associations. Expressing approval and disapproval is an activity that most humans engage in frequently. Spouses commend or criticize one another, teachers grade students, employers promote or demote workers, fans cheer a celebrity or boo a referee, and Facebook users check "likes." Status is not the only useful approach to understanding the sacred, nor is sacredness the only legitimate way to think of religion. Status and sacredness are, however, useful concepts and much more understandable to most modern people than most philosophical concepts. Hence, the next task is to define status and identify some of its crucial characteristics.

We need to make a slight diversion into social theory to explain what I have called the theory of status relations. I promise the diversion will be brief and relatively painless.

---

2. Durkheim, *Elementary Forms*.

3. There is much discussion and controversy about whether non-humans have agency, but this is an issue beyond the scope of this book.

RELIGION, SACREDNESS, AND STATUS

The Nature of Status and Sacredness

Status is the accumulated expressions of approval and disapproval directed toward a person, group, activity, object, idea, or anything else that actors evaluate. (I use the term "actors" because groups and organizations as well as individuals can be actors.) The status of something can certainly be mixed: some expressed approval and some disapproval. Alternatively, the very same person may be positive about some features of an actor or object and negative about others, and hence ambivalent or vacillating in the status they assign. Generally, however, a central tendency or average emerges overtime. Most contemporary people express more approval of physicians than they do of astrologers—not to speak of embezzlers or robbers. Status is not simply reducible to economic or political power, though they can be highly correlated, and one can be the source of the other.

Status is a particular form of power. Students and actors certainly perceive teachers and critics to have power over them, even though neither teachers nor critics use physical force or economic rewards; rather, they express approval or disapproval via grades or reviews. A high status can be a very useful resource even if it does not increase one's economic or political power; conversely, a low status can be a significant handicap even if one has wealth or political power.

Now we turn to the issue of how status differs from other resources.

Inexpansibility

Compared to economic or political power, status power is relatively inexpansible; it is basically a relative ranking. If everyone receives A's or a thousand Nobel Prizes are awarded annually, A's mean little and the prestige of the prizes decline. Inexpansibility has several important implications. First, inexpansibility affects *mobility* patterns; if someone moves up, someone else has to eventually move down.[4] Predictably, in systems where status is the central resource, mobility is very carefully regulated and restricted. Teenage nerds have a hard time joining the popular crowd. You cannot become a member of the National Academy of Sciences by filling out a form and sending in your dues; you have to be elected to membership by the existing members. Second, inexpansibility contributes to higher rates of *putdowns*; one way of staying up or moving up is to put others down. Consequently, teenagers are often quite mean to those they perceive to be competitors or upstarts. This is also why "critique" is such a central part of intellectual life, including the sciences. Third, inexpansibility interacts with the size of the group to affect the likelihood of *pluralism*. In a school with two hundred students, everyone knows most of the people in the "popular crowd" and often interacts regularly with them. In a school of two thousand, most students have no interaction with the popular crowd, may not know who they are, and have no hope of being admitted to this group. Instead, they form other subcultures with different values and symbols: punks, hippies, skaters, nerds, jocks, brains, etc. These groups usually reject the idea that the popular crowd is superior. So, the larger the social system or network, the more likely it is to become pluralistic with multiple subcultures. The less they have a shared concept about what is high status and low status, the more likely there will be conflict between groups. As we shall see, this tendency applies to churches as well as high schools.

Inalienability

Status is relatively inalienable. A robber can take your money or property, but they cannot simply appropriate your status; it is located in the minds of other people. Someone's status can change over time, but this requires changing the opinions of others. Consequently, once someone's status becomes established, it is relatively stable. Both the famous ex-quarterback and the notorious

---

4. In contrast, everyone in a society can become richer: the poor person becoming richer does not necessarily take money away from a rich person.

ex-embezzler are likely be affected by their past status. Ironically, the difficulty in changing the status of something can make it a very valuable resource. Those with new wealth or political influence often try to convert some of this new power into status in order to have a more secure resource, though this may take multiple generations. On the other hand, the difficulty in shedding a low status can motivate the deprived to form counter cultures with different norms and values.

The above characteristics specify some of the ways that status differs from other resources. The next two characteristics focus on the sources of status.

Conformity

Those who commonly deviate from core norms of a group usually have low status. Cowardly soldiers are looked down upon or court marshaled. Studying hard and making good grades usually improves a student's status among teachers, adults, and some peers; other peers may label the studious as "grinds" or "grade grubbers." Deviance may produce high status if it is seen as a valuable innovation, but those who already have high status are more likely to have their innovations appreciated. That conformity to a group's norms increases one's status is an obvious point. Slightly less obvious, those with high status often elaborate and complicate the norms to make it difficult for outsiders and upstarts. Examples of *elaboration* include religious purity or professional jargon. Fashion is frequently a form of elaboration—the high-status group regularly changes what is "in" so that others are always "behind." Alternatively, competition via fashion can be limited by absolute prohibitions against copying those of superior status; army privates had better not try to dress like generals.

Association

Associating with those of higher status tends to increase your status; associating with those of lower status tends to do the opposite. This is especially the case if the association involves an intimate expressive relationship. In virtually all cultures, eating and sex are key symbols of intimacy. Unsurprisingly, a central concern of teenagers is who eats with whom in the lunchroom and who is "hooking up" with whom. The boss may have a "working lunch" with lower-level employees, but seldom would she invite them to a dinner party. The boundaries of Indian castes are largely determined by who can marry whom and who eats with whom.

That is enough sociological theory for now. Status is not the only sociological concept that is of relevance to theology and later I will draw on other sociological terms. I have elaborated on the nature of status because I believe this provides a useful way to grasp the significance of sacredness and people's relationship to what they consider to be sacred. Before proceeding, I need to point to the importance of not exaggerating the role or significance of sociological explanations (or more generally of science) and the danger of dismissing other forms of human knowledge and experience.

Chapter 3

Meaning, Mystery, Magic, Metaphor, and Explanation

> *A religious symbol uses the material of ordinary experience in speaking of God, but in such a way that the ordinary meaning of the material used is both affirmed and denied. Every religious symbol negates itself in its literal meaning, but affirms itself in its self-transcending meaning.*
>
> —PAUL TILLICH[1]

Key Concepts

Meaning

THE WORLD RELIGIONS ATTEMPT to provide meaning to human life—both individual and collective. "Meaning" points to two different but related ideas. The first focuses on the accuracy of communication: "Do you understand what I am saying?" "Is this what this text means?" This concern arises in a number of contexts: following instructions, interpreting texts, marriage counseling, treaty and labor negotiations, information theory, etc.

The second concern is not primarily about the accuracy of communication, but rather whether something is meaningful. Prisoners and guards may have a high degree of mutual understanding, but neither may find their relationship or their shared

---
1. Tillich, *Systematic Theology*, 2:9.

social context very meaningful. Meaningfulness usually involves placing something relatively concrete in a broader context. Most of the particular events of the Hebrew Bible become meaningful in the context of the broader story of Yahweh calling Abraham and his descendants and the subsequent events described in the Old Testament. Across many societies, stories place a particular culture in the context of a broader understanding of creation. If human existence emerged by chance and will come to an end because the sun burns out (or because of a human-made ecological disaster), human history seems meaningless. A better scientific understanding of the cosmos, while desirable in itself, is not likely to offer much comfort when people face personal tragedies or the sun is exploding. Perhaps the most famous expression of such pessimism is by Shakespeare's Macbeth:

> To-morrow, and to-morrow, and to-morrow,
> Creeps in this petty pace from day to day,
> To the last syllable of recorded time;
> And all our yesterdays have lighted fools
> The way to dusty death. Out, out, brief candle!
> Life's but a walking shadow, a poor player,
> That struts and frets his hour upon the stage,
> And then is heard no more. It is a tale
> Told by an idiot, full of sound and fury,
> Signifying nothing. (*Macbeth*, act 5, scene 5, lines 19–28)

Macbeth is primarily talking about the meaninglessness of each individual's life. The depth of meaninglessness is even deeper if all of human history, the universe, and existence itself have no meaning, no larger story and context of which they are a part.

Such pessimism is often called nihilism, which certainly did not begin with Shakespeare. It has, however, always been a minority voice. Most people have thought that existence is not without meaning, but that it is in many respects mysterious.

MEANING, MYSTERY, MAGIC, METAPHOR, AND EXPLANATION

Mystery

Meaning is . . . a partial disclosure within a surrounding mystery . . .

—LANGDON GILKEY[2]

In the context of theology, mystery refers to something that is difficult to understand or beyond the typical modes of understanding. Just as humans—both as individuals and collectivities—have limited strength, power, and longevity, they have limited understanding. People may widen the scope of what they understand, but human understanding is never complete. Some of these limits are probably due to the limits of the brain, of language, and of the mind. Some are probably due to the sheer scope and complexity of the universe and its many components—including the tiny component we call earthly life.

There are different modes of understanding and reality. A physiologist may be able to describe in some detail the biology and the emotions associated with intense romantic love, but this does not capture the experience of the infatuated couple. The couple can try to tell others about the nature of their involvement, but such accounts only partially capture their existential experience. Novelists may draw on their own experience or the accounts of others to describe the emotions of fictional lovers. Neither the descriptions of the physiologist, the existential experience of the couple, their accounts of this experience, nor the accounts of novelists are wrong; they point to different kinds of human experience and understanding. One cannot be "reduced" to the other. All of these are, in their own way, "real." Fiction may not be real in the sense of reporting actual events, but it can certainly be real in its impact on people's emotions and their behavior. It is a mistake to think that only the accounts of the physiologist (or other "hard" sciences) are "real." The recognition of the limits of human knowledge, and that mystery is an inherent part of human experience

---

2. Gilkey, *On Niebuhr*, 56.

is important. These contribute to a humility that is good for both science and other forms of human understanding.

Magic

But an appreciation for mystery is not necessarily a lapse into magic. In their attempts to understand and shape the human experiences of contingency, powerlessness, and mystery, people have often resorted to magic. This was more the case in premodern periods, when less was known about causal relationships. Magic was commonly used in an attempt to affect worldly outcomes. The dictionary defines magic as having supernatural power over natural forces. Typically, magic involves using various symbolic rituals to affect some physical phenomena or the actions of other people. Examples included rituals to insure victory in battle or checking the alignment of the heavenly bodies before arranging marriages. Unsurprisingly, descriptions of magical procedures were often included in the textual accounts we have from the past, including the Bible. The long-term trend has been a decline in the use of magic both in religion and modern culture in general. Of course, magic has not disappeared; for example, many papers still publish daily astrological charts that purport to predict the future. To be creditable to modern educated people, religion must abandon magic without abandoning mystery.

Metaphor

Attempts to articulate religious mysteries are often expressed through metaphors and other figures of speech. When the New Testament describes Jesus as the "good shepherd," this is clearly metaphorical; there is no reason to think that Jesus spent much (or any) of his time herding sheep. On the other hand, he might literally have washed his disciples' feet, and almost certainly he "broke bread" with them. Yet the significance of these was not primarily in producing clean feet or reducing hunger. Rather, they symbolized

MEANING, MYSTERY, MAGIC, METAPHOR, AND EXPLANATION

and pointed to the ideals that Jesus was advocating. (Other figures of speech such as similes and irony are also used to communicate meanings and understandings.) In 1 Kings 19:11–12 the nature of God's power and some of her ways of relating to humans is expressed through a well-known passage about Elijah: "Now there was a great wind, so strong that it was splitting mountains and breaking rocks . . . but the Lord was not in the wind; and after the wind an earthquake, but the Lord was not in the earthquake; and after the earthquake a fire, but the Lord was not in the fire; and after the fire a sound of sheer silence . . ." Wind, earthquakes, fire, and silence are empirical phenomena, but here they are used as metaphors to suggest the nature of God's power. The parallel between forms of power and God's power are deliberately not precise. They are suggestive of his power, but recognize that it is inherently mysterious, because they refer to a different kind of truth and use a different mode of understanding.

In a similar spirit, I will draw upon various sociological concepts and ideas that may involve worldly social processes but can also point to something beyond literal social processes.

Metaphors can be tricky, especially translating metaphors from one language to another. For example, John Cobb argues that Jesus never addressed God as a king or monarch. He usually talked about God as "Abba," which is an intimate term similar to "Papa" in English. He suggests that a better translation of "kingdom of God" is "commonwealth of God." A commonwealth is a community founded for the common good. I will adopt this usage both because I find Cobb's argument convincing and because, with the exception of a few countries, kingdoms have been replaced my various kinds of republics, even though they may retain a figurehead king or queen.[3]

I am certainly not suggesting that we abandon the use of metaphors and other figures of speech, but that we need to be careful about the literalness we attribute to them.

---

3. Cobb, *Jesus' Abba*.

Explanation

Most social theories purport to explain why people behave the way they do. In a general sense, to "explain" means to make something clear or easy to understand. Explanations may involve showing the cause of a phenomenon. Within science there is debate about exactly what "explain" means. One of the most common meanings stresses the importance of prediction and parsimony; being able to predict future outcomes with the minimum number of theoretical concepts and previous knowledge. Another way of saying this is that a good explanation provides a linked description that enables the analysts to make predictions about events that have not yet occurred—or more accurately, have not been previously observed. Classically this involves being able to specify the necessary and sufficient conditions for a phenomenon to occur. In addition, the limits of the theory need to be stated. Psychoanalytic theory might be helpful in understanding and reducing the aggression of humans, and perhaps even pet dogs, but no reasonable person would suggest that insect pest should be given psychoanalysis in order to reduce their aggressiveness toward garden plants. Scientists are rightfully suspicious of theories that explain everything; they are usually tautologies.

Theology should have no objections to attempts to develop explanations that explain a wide variety of empirical phenomena. Darwin's theory of evolution helped us to see some of the key factors behind the emergence and eventual disappearance of various species. The theory reduced a lot of seemingly unrelated observations into a relatively simple general framework. This kind of reductionism should not be a problem for theology, but a reductionism that claims to reduce all forms of understanding to one particular perspective is another matter. There are many forms of reductionism and much disagreement about its implications.[4] We need to be skeptical when intellectuals start saying that there is only one legitimate mode of understanding. Claiming that something as complex as human relationships and human history—not

---

4. Mayes, *Explanation*; and Ney, *Reductionism*.

to speak of the nature of existence—is "nothing but" some physical or psychological process is, at best, arrogant.

Explain Away

To elaborate on the above point, being able explain something does not mean that this "explains away" all other reactions or understandings of a phenomenon. Being able to predict the time of an eclipse does not eliminate the sense of beauty and awe that people may gain from watching the event. Conversely, when a religiously inclined observer senses God's presence in an eclipse or in the Eucharist, this does not mean that God directly caused the eclipse or that the bread literally became the flesh of Christ. As William James pointed out more than a hundred years ago, explaining the origin of something does not necessarily speak to its value to human beings.[5] Good scientific explanations and the recognition of the importance of mystery are not mutually exclusive.[6]

The recognition of the inevitability of mystery is a form of humility. Good theology does not deny that science may change our understanding of the empirical world—including things described in sacred texts. In the realm of empirical phenomena, summarizing a lot of seemingly unrelated data within a more general theory is very useful—as long as we recognize that the abstractions that allow us to generalize focus on some things and ignores others. We need to constantly remind ourselves of the limits of our knowledge and of any one mode of knowledge. Certainly, good theology should try to constantly remind itself of the limits of what can be accomplished as it attempts to understand and relate to God.

What follows is not a sociology of theology in the sense of explaining the social sources of various theologies. Nor is it an attempt to explain away religious behavior as just another example of a more general social process. Rather, I am drawing on sociological

---

5. James, *Varieties of Religious Experience*, 45.

6. This argument has at least a "family resemblance" with the latter Ludwig Wittgenstein's argument that there are different language games and that description and science are not the only legitimate games.

concepts as useful metaphors and analogies for understanding some of the traditional topics of Christian theology. This is needed because many of the traditional understandings have become meaningless or unconvincing to many educated people.

Now I will turn to how sociological concepts and theories about status may help us to better understand the nature of sacredness without resorting to magic *and* without abandoning a sense of mystery and awe.

Special Characteristics of Sacredness

Most world religions have had notions of sacred divinities or gods, and of devils or evil spirits. One way to understand the nature of the sacred and of evil are to think of them as extreme cases of high and low status. Those of very high and very low status have special characteristics. Those of very high status usually find that many people want to interact with them

Even if such high-status people want to interact with ordinary people, they must ration the time they spend with others. This is both because there are only so many hours in a day and because too much contact with ordinary people tends to erode the status of those who are exalted. This is why those of very high status often have "retreats" to get a respite. At times, Jesus tried to escape from the crowds to renew his relationship with God or to instruct his disciples; often he was not successful in these attempts to withdraw.

Very high-status actors find it difficult to repair their status by upward associations since few are clearly superior—and those who are have busy schedules. This is why it is "lonely at the top." This distancing and rationing of access may make their lives seem mysterious. "Fans" can become curious, fascinated, and even obsessed about the details of the "private lives" of high-status people. Since most have no actual interaction with these superiors, the "hoi polloi" may try to create virtual relationships by grasping on to the bits of information that are revealed and the pseudo-information of rumor and gossip. Some of the stories in the Gospels and in

MEANING, MYSTERY, MAGIC, METAPHOR, AND EXPLANATION

the Islamic Hadith probably originate from this kind of behavior by religious devotees. In contemporary society, fan magazines and TV programs about the "rich and famous" are a good example of this. The devotees and fans of such celebrities may call them "gods." Some celebrities are held in awe and even "worshipped"; a few may even become "immortal" and take on a sacred and holy quality. John Lennon is one example of a modern celebrity that could become a quasi-god. Historically, a number of highly admired people have literally become deified. Pointing out some of the likely social processes that were involved may help to explain the content of sacred scripture, reducing the tendency to see such behavior as magical or supernatural. This does not "explain away" the significance of these stories—much less the limits of human knowledge or the legitimacy of a sense of mystery and awe.

Alliances with the Divine: Antidote, Poison, or Tranquilizer?

Everyone faces disappointments and frustrations; even the most successful and privileged eventually die. This is one reason most of us eagerly seek moments when others express approval of us. But as the above discussion indicated, such accomplishments easily slip into pride, arrogance, and a tendency to put others down.

Human pride and arrogance can be reduced by the recognition of human finitude and the limits of human power, but this highlights our vulnerability. How do we cope with this relative powerlessness and finitude? One antidote to powerlessness and vulnerability is to seek alliances with more powerful actors. Such alliances are a particular kind of social relationship. Examples include younger and older friends, students and their mentors, and employees and their superiors. Such alliances were the core of feudal systems: for protection and other resources, a person became a vassal of a more powerful person.

Alliances can also be made with super-humans—that is, gods—with the hope that they will protect and support us. Across cultures, the nature of the alliances and the character of the gods vary significantly. Some relationships with deities are little more than quid pro quo exchanges: "we'll make sacrifices if you bring the rains." In ancient Israel the alliance was conceived of as an ongoing covenant with Yahweh: more like a long-term marriage than an exchange in the market place. The New Testament faith still involves an alliance with a superior, as indicated by the phrase "Jesus is Lord" (e.g., 1 Corinthians 12:3; Romans 10:9), but this alliance is a more intimate and intense. As noted above, when Jesus addressed God he usually called him Abba, that is, Papa.[7]

The inexpansibility of status means that when people assign extraordinarily high status to gods, this results in the demotion of humans. This is even more the case in monotheistic religions. Usually such religions have a concept of divine law, which is to guide human actions. The high status of the god and the sense that she is the origin of human morality provide the grounds for social and personal humility.[8] This is typically expressed through various kinds of rituals including purification, confession, and worship. The person who regularly confesses their sins of both commission and omission is probably more likely to be aware of the dangers of arrogance and pride—which is not to say that they escape them completely. People who worship a monotheistic god usually recognize that humanity is neither the beginning nor the end of creation. This effect is probably accentuated if God's status is considered inalienable. God is not only superior—holy, powerful, awesome; God is also sacred and dependable—like a rock, a refuge, a fortress. Thus, the inexpansibility and inalienability of status means that the recognition of divinity can be an antidote for human pride and arrogance. These positive effects are accentuated when people publicly share their sense of finitude and their awe of the divine.[9] Collective worship is the most common way to express this.

---

7. Cobb, *Jesus' Abba*.

8. The relationship between religion and morality is a complex matter that has long been debated. For a sketch of how philosophers have dealt with this issue, See Hare, *"Religion and Morality."*

9. People can also make alliances with supernatural beings who may be

MEANING, MYSTERY, MAGIC, METAPHOR, AND EXPLANATION

But the antidote can become a poison. When humans too closely identify their own insecurities, desires and efforts with a divine will, it can become an excuse for the most horrendous kinds of injustices and atrocities. The past and present persecutions and wars, justified in the name of religion, make this clear. Opponents come to be considered not just wrongheaded or selfish, but evil. Historical examples include the Islamic conquest of North Africa, the Christian Crusades, and much of Western imperialism. Contemporary examples are the Catholic-Protestant conflicts of Northern Ireland, the ongoing clashes in the Middle East, and persecution of various groups in Africa and Asia. (Divinities, devils and religion, however, are certainly not the only way of justifying injustices and atrocities. The persecution and atrocities committed by avowedly secular groups make this evident.[10])

More subtly, alliances with deities can become a tranquilizer. Devotees can become insensitive or even oblivious to the needs of others—and take on a sense of self-satisfied conformism. Contemporary critics of religion point to the conventionality of religious people, but this is hardly new. The most influential theologian of the eighteenth century, Friedrich Schleiermacher, put it this way, "At all times but few have discerned religion itself, while millions, in various ways, have been satisfied to juggle with its trappings."[11] Ludwig Feuerbach, the nineteenth-century critic of religion, is even more offended by conventional religion: "Faith gives man a peculiar sense of his own dignity and importance. The believer finds him distinguished above other men,

---

thought of as powerful, but who have a negative or ambivalent status. These beings are seldom associated with Divine law or human morality. Such figures are typically portrayed as devils, evil spirits, witches, fallen angels, gods that are indifferent to humans or even see them as play things.

10. The Reign of Terror during the French Revolution, the expelling or killing Native Americans and the appropriation of Mexican territory in the name of Manifest Destiny, the Nazi Holocaust, the Soviet gulag, the Maoist Cultural Revolution, and the Cambodian genocide by the Khmer Rouge are only the most obvious examples of atrocities carried out in the name of various forms of secularism.

11. Schleiermacher, *On Religion*, 1.

exalted above the natural man; he knows himself to be a person of distinction, in the possession of peculiar privileges; believers are aristocrats, unbelievers are plebeians."[12]

The key point is that a sense of one's relationship to the divine can help to reduce pride and egotism, but it can also make one arrogant or oblivious. When arrogance becomes the characteristic of not just individuals, but of groups, the result may be the worst kind of religious conflict and war. But this is not unique to religions. As the discussion of sin will suggest, nearly all relationships and all forms of power can become distorted and destructive. But neither religious individualism nor forcing religion out of the public sphere is the answer. Avoiding social relationships and seeking complete self-reliance in the profane world is a mistake. So is spiritual self-reliance—which is characteristic of many forms of meditation. For this causes us to overlook the potential redemptive power of a relationship with the Divine. And as we shall see, relating to the Divine is most successful when it is a collective project.

The Nature of God's Power and Love

It is helpful to begin the discussion of God's power with a discussion of human power. At the root of most kinds of social power is the ability to sanction others. For political power the fundamental sanction is force. Economic power is based on withholding or providing goods and services. Status power is based on others' expressions of approval and disapproval. Societies and groups vary in the relative importance and legitimacy of different forms of power. Aggressive societies may come close to worshipping force. As an Old Testament prophet says of the Babylonians, ". . . their own might is their god" (Habakkuk 1:11).[13] In the Soviet

---

12. Feuerbach, *Essence of Christianity*.

13. The context of this telling phrase is Habakkuk 1:6–11:

For indeed I am raising up the Chaldeans,
A bitter and hasty nation
Which marches through the breadth of the earth,
To possess dwelling places that are not theirs.

MEANING, MYSTERY, MAGIC, METAPHOR, AND EXPLANATION

Union force was more hidden, but nonetheless political power was central, and organized force was crucial to this power. In most capitalist societies, and especially the U.S., economic power has the most legitimacy and the most effect in shaping of societal decisions. In traditional India, status in the form of caste was a central form of power that significantly shaped the society for at least two thousand years. Of course, status was not irrelevant in the Soviet Union, and wealth was important in traditional India, but status could not turn a Russian movie star into a Politburo member or a rich Untouchable into a Brahmin.

Approvals and disapprovals, which make up status, can be expressed toward particular kinds of behavior, individuals, groups, objects, etc. Another way of saying this is that expressions of approval and disapproval are sanctions, which can be positive as well as negative.

There are examples in the Bible of divine force. God used plagues, including killing all the Egyptians' first-born children, to persuade the pharaoh to allow the exodus. In order to induce the Hebrews to continue their journey, God offered them goods and services: manna to quench their hunger and pillars of cloud and fire to guide them (Exodus 13:21 and 16:35). After Jesus' death

---

They are terrible and dreadful;
Their judgment and their dignity proceed from themselves.
Their horses also are swifter than leopards,
And more fierce than evening wolves.
Their chargers charge ahead;
Their cavalry comes from afar;
They fly as the eagle that hastens to eat.
"They all come for violence;
Their faces are set like the east wind.
They gather captives like sand.
They scoff at kings,
And princes are scorned by them.
They deride every stronghold,
For they heap up earthen mounds and seize it.
Then his mind changes, and he transgresses;
He commits offense,
Ascribing this power to his god."

and resurrection, the early church experienced God's power via the Holy Spirit. In Pentecostal churches this has taken the form of various types of ecstasy such as speaking in tongues. But in most other branches of the church, God's means of using his power has been less dramatic—though charismatic movements have emerged even in traditions noted for their ritual and hierarchy (e.g., Roman Catholic and Anglican churches).

How might we conceive of God's power in ways that modern people would recognize and find creditable? Process theology attempts to address this problem by reconceptualizing God. God is not an unchanging omnipotent being. Rather, like the creation and like humans, God is in the process of becoming. God is affected by ongoing relationships with the universe, including humans. This is not unlike the way that humans are in the process of becoming because of their ongoing relationship with others and with God. In a sense, both God and humans are pilgrims.

God's power neither violates the laws of nature nor operates through the commands of an all-powerful king. Rather, process theology speaks of God luring humans toward behavior that helps to redeem them and the world in which they live. The virtue of this imagery is that it conceives of God as actively seeking reconciled relationships with humans.

Nonetheless, I have a problem with the language and imagery of process theology, especially the notion of luring.[14] Since boyhood I have been a fisherman, primarily a bass fisherman who uses artificial lures.[15] Consequently the idea of God using lures and hooks has

---

14. Process theology is derived from the complex philosophical ideas drawn from Alfred N. Whitehead and elaborated on by others. I will not try to summarize or discuss these issues—more than the core ideas already mentioned. Such a discussion would be a major tangent. I doubt, however, that process theology's abstract and complex vocabulary will become central and meaningful to most churches. Process theology has existed for about ninety years, but I think it is fair to say relatively few ministers ground their sermons in this perspective and even fewer laypeople are aware of this perspective. Thus, for all its philosophical virtues it has had little impact on the typical church members understanding of their faith.

15. I hope my animal rights friends can find it in their heart to forgive me. I did give up hunting many years ago.

never appealed to me. More to the point, "lure" implies deception, manipulation, and ensnarement—it seems lurid.

Recall that I suggested it is useful to think of God as that which is sacred and of sacredness as the ultimate form of status. Hence, we might think of God's power as having parallels with the way very high-status people influence us. Most of us find those whom we admire attractive; we want to associate with them. This is one of the appeals of being religious; associating with the one who has supreme status. If we truly admire someone, we tend to adopt their norms and their perspective on the world, especially if they actively try to persuade us of the superiority of their worldview. God can also influence us with his expressions of disapproval and approval. When we do things that are wrong, we believe that God judges us and expresses disapproval. On the other hand, we believe that again and again God has forgiven us and encouraged us to return to his ways. So, God is not only attractive, she is active. He repeatedly invites us into relationship with him and tries to persuade us to follow in his way. However much our actions may receive her disapproval, we have a sense that if we repent and try again, she will approve of us and restore our status as members of the Commonwealth of God. So, God's power is exercised primarily by attracting, inviting, and persuading us—primarily by loving us; this is the gospel's good news. As a modern Presbyterian statement of faith says:

> Like a mother who will not forsake her nursing child,
> like a father who runs to welcome the prodigal home,
> God is faithful still[16]

But there is an important caveat. Such divine seeking and influence are to a significant degree contingent upon the status we attribute to God. The more that we exalt God in regular worship and prayer, the more power he has to shape our lives. The wonder is the constancy of her love for us in light of flawed and inconstant worship. Such worship and prayer, however, requires that we acknowledge a fundamental human flaw: the tendency to exalt

---
16. Presbyterian Church (U.S.A.), "Brief Statement of Faith."

ourselves and diminish others. This is the subject we will consider next in our discussion of sin. Our recognition of sin makes his love for us all the more mysterious and amazing.

Now we turn to some of the classic doctrines of the church to see how status and other sociological concepts might help us to better understand such doctrines and to make what they are trying to express more creditable to contemporary people.

Chapter 4

Some Classical Doctrines in a New Language

... new attempts to formulate religious understandings are likely to be most valuable when they enrich and supplement what has been thought in the past.

—Edward Leroy Long[1]

THE PURPOSE OF THIS chapter is to take some of the common theological doctrines and to restate them, in ways that are more understandable to contemporary people, using primarily sociological concepts.

Sin

... if the task of writing a systematic theology began explicitly with the most fundamental emotional concerns... it would address the way evil insidiously creeps into every human life.

—Margaret D. Kamitsuka et al.[2]

---

1. Long, *Nature and Future of Christianity*, 82.
2. Kamitsuka et al., "Sin and Evil."

In common parlance "sin" means a serious fault or an offense against a religious or moral law. The Christian concept of sin includes these notions but refers to a much more fundamental problem. Humans are seen as inherently flawed and inclined to evil. To make matters worse, what is initially motivated by good intensions frequently becomes a matter of self-glorification. Am I writing this book to help myself and others better understand the Christian faith? Or is it to take pride in being a published author and hopefully to receive praise from others? Certainly, it is both, but as a sinful human I almost certainly exaggerate the first and minimize the second. This notion of sin—as a tragic condition of human life—is controversial and offensive to many contemporary people.[3]

How might sociological concepts help us to better grasp the Christian understanding of sin? Evolutionary biology points to the drive of all organisms to eat and reproduce—usually at the expense of other organisms. The aggression involved in "the survival of the fittest" is certainly one source of conflict, exploitation, and domination. But our biological drives are not primarily what the Bible means by sin.

Adam and Eve were allowed to freely eat of the garden—*except* for the tree of the knowledge of good and evil (Genesis 2:16–17). So, neither scarcity nor predatory behavior was the root of sin. Rather, the serpent entices Eve to ignore this one prohibition by saying, "You will not die; for God knows that when you eat of it your eyes will be opened, and you will be like God" (Genesis 3:3). When they had eaten they became aware that they were naked, and they hid themselves because they were ashamed and afraid.

In this passage the first concrete consequence of "the fall" was not literal death, but shame and fear. These emotions point toward the root causes of sin. The opposite of shame is pride, and the height of pride is the attempt to "be like God." The opposite of fear is a sense of security that results in assurance and trust; that

---

3. Among modern theologians it is Reinhold Niebuhr who has most emphasized this conception of sin. He did not, however, adequately elaborate the source of this condition in terms that are meaningful to postmodern people.

SOME CLASSICAL DOCTRINES IN A NEW LANGUAGE

is, you have faith. Theologians as diverse as Augustine, Aquinas, Calvin, and Niebuhr have pointed to pride and lack of faith as the elemental sources of sin. Granted, some emphasized one more than the other.

Words like pride and shame assume some concept of judging and evaluation, of expressing approval and disapproval, that is, judgments to distinguish best from worst, good from evil. As I pointed out in the previous chapter, the accumulation of such expressions is the source of status. Most people care deeply about their social status and their self-esteem. Inflated self-images can lead to overblown and even delusional notions of greatness. Conversely, low social status and self-esteem can lead to withdrawal, passivity, and even suicide.

All organisms, including humans, struggle to obtain needed resources—food, shelter, mates. For humans there is the additional and, in some ways, more fundamental struggle: the striving for status—for self-respect and respect from others. As discussed above, status has two somewhat unique characteristics: inexpansibility and inalienability. *Inexpansibility* creates an inherent scarcity that leads to endless striving for superiority and a strong tendency to make others feel inferior. That is, humans tend to actively create pride and shame. If people are assigned a low status, they often withdraw, rejecting the dominant status system and creating an alternative system. Usually these counter status systems imagine themselves as fundamentally different. For example, they take pride in not being prideful—or more accurately, not being prideful about the same things. For example, rather than taking pride in wealth and having the "latest stuff," a group may take pride in poverty and asceticism. Some groups advocate being accepting and non-judgmental, but this results in low status for those who are judgmental and high status for those who are not. This is not to deny that people and groups vary in how preoccupied they are with their status, and how aggressively they pursue superiority, but all are fundamentally prideful and anxious. This results in not only individuals seeking to be superior by treating others as inferior, but also the creation of status systems that accentuate tendencies toward pride and shame.

35

While certain levels of self-respect and pride in particular accomplishments may be appropriate, we tend to ignore how easily and frequently our self-respect lapses into the denigration of others or inflates into self-glorification that turns us into would-be demigods—the fundamental form of sin.

As much as the inexpansibility of status may lead to sin, *inalienability* results in social and personal identities being very difficult to change. Having graduated from Harvard or Oxford gives you a certain kind of respect even if you do not have a distinguished career; being an "ex-con" is likely to reduce your job prospects for the rest of your life. Such relatively inalienable social identities tend to produce self-images in which pride and shame are deeply embedded. Even more problematic are inalienable characteristics that are largely inherited such as gender, skin color, and language. The result is that sin becomes built into the social order and because of inalienability is extremely difficult to overcome.

As just suggested, sin operates on both the individual and the collective level. At the individual level we know of many "saints" who, though they have not become sinless, have to some degree avoided extreme forms of pride and insecurity. Many have done this by opening themselves to a transforming intimacy with God—something all Christians are called upon to do. While some nation-states are less aggressive more benign than others, none can be considered saintly. At the collective level, the inclinations of groups toward insecurity and pride are even more intense. A politician or a corporation's CEO who always "turns the other cheek" and ignores the interests of their own collectivity is likely to lose their leadership position.

Collective sin can be more appalling than that of individuals. Wars for national expansion are all too common: Russia taking over the Crimea and eastern Ukraine, the Germans invading Austria and Poland, and the U.S. appropriating the lands of Native Americans and annexing much of the Southwest from Mexico. These are only three obvious examples. Even more appalling are the three hundred years of American slavery, the Holocaust, and numerous cases of ethnic "cleansing," often involving the systematic killing of

SOME CLASSICAL DOCTRINES IN A NEW LANGUAGE

civilians. Because of inalienability, collective sin can be even more difficult to avoid or change. This is evident in the long history of patriarchy, institutionalized racism, and chauvinistic nationalism. Such patterns of discrimination require not merely the transformation of an individual, or even a large number of individuals, but of changing the "normal," taken-for-granted routines of daily life. In some respects, it is like asking people to change their mother tongue. The recognition of this does not excuse defending or sustaining unjust patterns, but it does help to recognize the depths of our collective sin. Even disadvantaged or exploited groups are not free from collective sin, as the stories of the Hebrews' exodus from Egypt and their brutal conquest of Palestine make all too clear. The exploited can quickly slip into self-righteous victims and become the exploiters. Such tendencies are not restricted to the past but are present in modern societies.

The tendencies toward exalting self and degrading others are central to what is referred to as "original sin." Original sin is not about something that happened in a mythical garden. In part, "original sin" is rooted in the fight of all organisms to survive and reproduce. For more complex species, this may include the sexual lust that is part of the drive to reproduce one's own kind. More importantly, sin is about the efforts of humans to be superior to others and our willingness to put others down to gain or maintain our superiority—and the insecurity that is both the source and the product of these strivings. It is our efforts to be like God.

Many forms of secularism in effect turn the human species into "God." In most cases they turn a particular subculture of humans into the only legitimate creators of meaning and the ultimate judge of the good, the true, and the beautiful. They deny the possibility of meaning other than that created by human beings, and hence most of the universe is meaningless.

This arrogance has led to many of the tragedies of human history. The problem is not that humans have the ability to evaluate, for this is the source of our concepts of the good, the true, and the beautiful. Rather, the problem is our insecurity about how we will be evaluated by ourselves, other humans, and God. This insecurity derives from our lack of faith in God's love. Anxiety about our own worldly and spiritual status leads to our willingness to exaggerate our own virtue, knowledge, and tastes, and to denigrate others.

Understanding sin in the above manner acknowledges that humans have both freedom and responsibility for sin.[4] At the same time, this recognizes that our inclination to abuse others and to play God—the core of the biblical understanding of sin—is deeply embedded at both the individual and the collective level. (I will deal more extensively with the problem of evil at the end of chapter 8.)

Incarnation

A primary concern of the disciples and the early church was, "Who is this Jesus?" Discussions of the nature and person of Jesus are generally referred to as Christology. At the center of Christology is the concept of incarnation.

The names and titles used for Jesus in the New Testament include Christ (meaning Messiah), Son of God, Son of Man, Lord, Savior, and God. After the crucifixion, it was clear that Jesus was not the hoped-for Jewish Messiah that would oust the Romans and establish a Jewish kingdom. Clearly his apostles and disciples felt he was something special: someone who was in some sense sacred. But was he a man or a God? I will not try to recount the varied and complex arguments of the church fathers about the nature of Jesus. There are many dimensions to these debates, but certainly a primary issue can be grasped by pointing to two polar concepts. What came to be called *adoptionism* thought of Jesus as a human being that God adopted as his son. Various versions differ in the degree to which Jesus becomes a god. They also vary in the time of the adoption, for example at his baptism vs. the crucifixion vs.

---

4. "Agency" (rather than "freedom" and "responsibility") is the "in" word to express humans' ability to make choices that are not determined by their past or social context and to act on such choices. There is an extensive and complex literature dealing with both the meaning of agency and its various uses. See, for example, Schlosser, *Agency*.

his ascension. *Docetism* is the other pole. The word comes from the Greek *dokein*, "to seem." In this view Jesus was actually God in the form of an apparition or phantom. These polar positions became defined as "heresies," that is, poor ways of understanding the nature of Jesus. Much of early theology struggled to find a middle ground. This was a major focus of such church fathers as Justin Martyr (100–165), Clement (c. 150–215), Origen (185–254), Athanasius (328–373), Theodore (c. 350–428), Cyril of Alexandria (412– 444). While Arius (250–336), has not been an orthodox church father, he also played a role in this debate.

The degree to which Jesus was considered to be God was important for a number of reasons. One of these was whether he should be worshipped: yes if he was God, no if he was only an adopted human. Another reason was the role he plays in salvation. If he is only a prophet, then humans must conform to the law. This means we still have to "fix things" ourselves. If he is God seeking us out and willingly associating with us in an intimate relationship, then this very relationship transforms us.

The idea of a god incarnating himself in virgin young women and producing a man-god increasingly seems nonsensical to modern humans, or at the very least an inadequate metaphor. Two theologians who grappled with this issue in relatively modernist ways were Rudolf Bultmann (1884–1976) and Paul Tillich. Bultmann asserted that in a scientific age, belief in miracles is impossible. Hence, much of the New Testament account needs to be recognized as myth. While these myths may have been useful for religious faith, for modern people such stories must be "demythologized." What matters is not what actually happened, but the effect of Jesus on his disciples and the early church. Jesus's saving message (i.e., the *kerygma*), expressed in his proclamations and preaching, is what matters. For Tillich, Jesus Christ was the symbol of the presence of God. He symbolizes the potential for what a human can be; he is the symbol of what Tillich called "the New Being."[5]

---

5. These very brief summaries of Bultmann and Tillich do not do justice the full complexity of their arguments, but they do, I believe, capture their core notions.

While these accounts are better than asking modern people to believe in virgin births, I suspect that they may place too heavy an emphasis on human language and rationality. Humans do not "live by bread alone," but neither do they live by language alone. Language is a relatively late development in the evolutionary process. We are shaped not only by culture and language, but also by physical processes that are prelinguistic. Some of these are inherited; some are shaped by our past practices; some are both. Young animals do not play because they cognitively understand that it is good for their development; at least in part, play is built into their genes. Certain forms of religious behavior, such as bodily movements that indicate respect, seem at least partly genetic. A sense of awe at great beauty or power may be another example. Linking the physical and symbolic is important for both social science and theology. There is an increasing recognition that much of social theory is too cognitive. Our behavior is assumed to be due to "rational choices." Rationality means we are able to give creditable reasons for our choices, and more generally, for whatever we affirm. Yet, much of behavior comes from deeply embedded inclinations. Christian theology has often associated sin with bad habits. For example, Augustine moans, "For the law of sin is the tyranny of habit, by which the mind is drawn and held, even against its will."[6] But habits can be good, and such a notion is relevant to the concept of the incarnation. This is not, however, to deny the importance of human cognitive capacities and rationality.

Here I will draw on the sociological concept of *habitus*. Among sociologists the term was popularized by the very influential French sociologist Pierre Bourdieu (1930–2002). It has become a cliché that tends to be over used, but nonetheless points to something important. It recognizes that much of behavior is not based on consciously sorting through the possible alternatives and rationally choosing the most effective means to some desirable outcome. Much of our behavior is more like our quick reaction to seeing a child in danger or the reflexive moves of a good athlete. They come from long-established habits that are inculcated in both

---

6. Augustine of Hippo, *Confessions*, 123.

our minds and our bodies. (One of the key perspectives on ethics, virtue ethics, draws on similar ideas.)[7]

One way of thinking about the incarnation is to understand Jesus as someone who had deeply internalized the will of God, not only in his mind but *also in his body*. This was reflected in both his message and his life. He "instinctively" identified with and ministered to the outcasts of this time and place. Concepts such as *habitus* help us understand the centrality and importance of the incarnation—of embodiment—without having to resort to magical thinking.[8]

In addition to the personal attributes that caused people to attribute divinity to Jesus, there is the social process, found in many complex societies, that tends to deify a limited number of very high-status people. An obvious non-Christian example is Siddhārtha Gautama, who became the Buddha. The designation of historical figures as saints is a lesser degree of deification. This is characteristic of the Roman Catholic and Orthodox Churches as well as Shia Islam. A still yet weaker version of this process is the near-sacred status attributed to a few recent political figures: George Washington, Simon Bolivar, Mustafa Kemal Ataturk, Vladimir Lenin, Mahatma Gandhi, Mao Zedong. The historians and ideologues of later periods (and the collective memories they try to create) can increase or diminish the sacredness of historical person and the degree of adoration they receive. For example, Lenin and Mao have diminished in stature as their homelands

---

7. There are parallels with various approaches to ethics. Virtue ethics claims we are more likely to engage in moral behavior if we concentrate on cultivating virtuous inclinations. This is often contrasted with deontological ethics that concentrates on the character of the behavior itself and rules to guide this, or consequentialist ethics that focus on whether the outcomes of an action are good or bad, with less attention to either an actor's intensions or the means they use to accomplish an outcome. This brief description leaves out the variations and subtleties within each tradition. In fact, most moral actors draw on various combinations of these perspectives.

8. To recognize prelinguistic forms of motivation and action is not to glorify all forms of such drives and emotions. This is the tendency of nineteenth-century Romanticism's view of "life forces." In its most distorted form it became various forms of fascism.

have largely abandoned socialism. In contemporary societies, some celebrities can come close to being considered "gods" by their most ardent fans.

But why do humans see god-like qualities in some people? Often such charismatic persons articulate a new kind of consciousness. Usually this new consciousness both calls into question the status quo—and especially the existing relations of dominance and subordination—and offers hope for a new and better future. This vision typically advocates both a new social order and a new way of thinking about the inevitable stresses and tragedies of life, especially death. This is why phrases like "the kingdom of God," "the commonwealth of God," "the peace of Christ," and "the resurrection" have been so central to the Christian gospel. These concepts take on a sacred quality of their own and help transform Jesus into the Christ.

All of this is to suggest that at least many of the individual characteristics of Jesus and his transformation into the Son of God can be partially understood in relatively "naturalistic" terms. This is not to be dismissive of the concept of incarnation. Incarnation expresses in powerful, metaphorical terms the extent to which Jesus revealed and embodied what we mean by God and God's revelation of herself.

Contemporary process theologian Catherine Keller argues that incarnation should not be restricted to Jesus Christ: ". . . the core doctrine of Christianity, the incarnation, celebrates the embodiment of God in the world. . . . It is not just a matter of the single incarnation, but of an enfleshment always and everywhere taking place, and always different."[9]

Other theologians, especially in the mystic tradition, have made similar arguments. Richard Rohr puts it this way: "God is not just saving people; God is saving all of creation . . . We could call it the primordial 'Christification' or anointing of the universe at Creation. This is not pantheism (God is everything), but panentheism (God is in everything!)."[10]

---

9. Keller, *On the Mystery*, 52.
10. Rohr, *Christification of the Universe*.

SOME CLASSICAL DOCTRINES IN A NEW LANGUAGE

I take these assertions to mean that metaphors that refer only to ways of transforming how humans think about the world are by themselves inadequate. We must transform not just our conscious minds, but also the more or less automatic habits of our whole being. More traditional ways of expressing this incorporation of what Jesus represents into human selves include the biblical phrase "in Christ," or "in him." (An example is Acts 17:28: "For 'in Him we live and move and have our being'....") Moreover, the incarnation involves transforming not just humans but the sacralization of the whole universe in the sense that "God is in everything." This is why the seemingly anachronistic notion of incarnation is still useful.

The Trinity

Who can understand the omnipotent Trinity? And yet who does not speak about it, if indeed it is of it that he speaks? Rare is the soul who, when he speaks of it, also knows of what he speaks.

—AUGUSTINE OF HIPPO[11]

The Trinity has been one of the core concepts of Christian theology. In the relatively small city in which I live, there are at least three churches that have the word Trinity in their official name. This is a pattern found around the world. Yet the meaning of the Trinity has been ambiguous and controversial since its initial formulation in the fourth century AD.

Before proceeding to a reinterpretation drawing on sociological concepts, a bit of history is required. The debates over the relationship of God and Jesus, which are reflected in the idea of incarnation, soon became linked to arguments about the role and nature of the Holy Spirit. The Hebrew word *ruach* appears in the Old Testament more than three hundred times, in phrases such as "wind [*ruach*] from God swept over the face of the earth" (Genesis 1:2) and "the spirit [*ruach*] of the Lord came upon him" (Jude

---

11. Augustine of Hippo, *Confessions*, 236.

3:10). The concept of spirit is also important in the New Testament, most obviously in the account of Pentecost, when the Spirit (*pneuma*) descends upon the apostles. In both Hebrew and Greek, the word for "spirit" is often associated with the breath of life or described as a mighty wind. According to the Gospel of Matthew, new converts should be baptized "in the name of the Father and of the Son, and of the Holy Spirit" (28:19).

During the first four centuries of the early church there were ongoing debates about both the nature of Jesus and the relationship between God, Jesus, and the Holy Spirit. In an attempt to resolve disputes over how these relationships should be understood, a council of bishops met first in 325 AD in Nicaea (Turkey) and again in Constantinople (Istanbul, Turkey) in 381 AD. They declared that Jesus was not initially a historical person, but an aspect of the Deity from the beginning of time. According to this belief he was not adopted or made by God—for this would suggest that he was a secondary or derived aspect of the deity. To stress this point, they came up with the formula that Jesus Christ was "begotten, not made, being of one substance with the Father."

One part of this formula stressed the unity of the Trinity: Father, Son, and Holy Spirit were of one substance. "One substance" is the translation of *homoousia*, from *homos* (meaning the same) and *ousia* (meaning substance, essence, being). The other part of the formula stressed the distinctiveness of each aspect of the Trinity. There were three persons: Father, Son, and Holy Spirit. The Latin version uses the word *persona*, which initially referred to masks worn by actors on the stage. (Over time *persona* increasingly came to mean personality or character, which is one source of confusion.) Another imagery is that of the first, second, and third person in grammar.[12] Hence, the standard orthodox formula became "one substance, three persons."

---

12. John Hare explains it this way: "The church had to explain how the Father, the Son and the Holy Spirit could be distinct and yet not three different gods. They used, in Latin, the term *persona*, which means 'role' but which was also used by the grammarians to distinguish what we call 'first person, second person and third person' pronouns and verb-forms. The same human being can be first person 'I', second person 'you', and third person 'he' or 'she', depending

SOME CLASSICAL DOCTRINES IN A NEW LANGUAGE

Significant variations in the interpretations of the Nicaea formula soon emerged. While virtually all rejected any notion of three gods, some emphasized the distinctiveness of the three "persons" and some emphasized their unity. I will not try to cover the array of complex arguments and debates but will again focus on what might be considered the polar views. *Modalism* argued that there was only one god that revealed herself in three different modes.[13] Some emphasized a functional modalism: Father as lawgiver, Son as savior, and a Spirit that gives sanctification and eternal life. Others advocated a chronological modalism: first as Father, then as Son, and finally as the Holy Spirit. Modalism was declared a heresy in large measure because it would mean that God, in the person of Jesus, had suffered at the crucifixion. This would seriously compromise the (largely Greek) idea that God was *omnipotent* (i.e., all powerful) and *impassible* (i.e., incapable of suffering or of experiencing pain, inaccessible to injury). *Tritheism* was the other extreme, which saw the three persons as separate entities who, though in fellowship with each other, were independent, equal, and autonomous beings.[14]

Most seminary students and ordained clergy find it challenging to understand these various arguments; even fewer draw upon them in preaching, or pastoral counseling. The popular British Methodist Colin Morris claimed, "Any preacher with good sense will call in sick on Trinity Sunday."[15] To the laity, much of this sounds like phrases from a foreign language, which they may have heard many times, can repeat, and may be

---

on the relations in which he or she stands. The doctrine of the Trinity comes to be understood in terms of three persons, one God, with the persons standing in different relations to each other." Hare, "Religion and Morality."

13. Also known as Sabellianism.

14. A variety of the tritheism issue was the *filioque* debate between the Eastern and Western church. In the Nicene Creed the Eastern church held that the Spirit proceeded "from the Father" while the Western church proclaimed that the Spirit proceeded from only the Father or from the Father and the Son. For our purposes it is not necessary to elaborate on the complicated history of this issue.

15. Quoted in Willimon, "Trinity."

45

comforting because of their familiarity, but have only the vaguest idea of their theological significance.

How might we draw on sociological concepts help to understand the unity and diversity of God? Nearly everyone is familiar with the idea of multiple social roles: the same person can be a lawyer, a spouse, a parent, a city council member, a church deacon, etc. This parallels the multiple ways we experience God: as a Father or Mother, as Jesus, and as the Holy Spirit—and perhaps in other ways and forms. That is, I am suggesting a multidimensional understanding of God. Clearly, drawing on the concept of social role is a form of modalism. This is, however, less a problem for contemporary theology because increasingly the omnipotence and the impassibility of God have been called into question. Jürgen Moltmann has famously argued that the Christian God is a god who suffers when people suffer, rather than a remote power that is unaffected by what happens to his devotees.[16]

Given that much of theology has in many ways already revised the understanding of omnipotence, omniscience, and impassibility, this removes many of the problematic aspects of modalism. (As we shall see, it also suggests a way to better understand the problem of evil.)

I see no reason, however, why God must be limited to only three roles. If we think about our personal relationships, others often play multiple roles, or roles that have many dimensions.[17] My wife and I have been married for many years. The roles she has played include daily companion, meal partner, lover, mother of our children, cook, shopper, director of music in a church, sharer of many memories, honest critic, tormentor, and victim of my many failings. Of course, our intimate human relationships are not exactly the same as those we have with God. Nonetheless, our relationship to the Divine is often complex and multilayered.

---

16. Moltmann, *Crucified God*.

17. In the sociological literature a distinction is sometime drawn between social positions (e.g., mother, professional engineer, citizen) and the multiple roles that may be involved in filling a particular position. The more common usage, which I will use, is to treat "social roles" and "social positions" as synonyms.

SOME CLASSICAL DOCTRINES IN A NEW LANGUAGE

For purposes of simplification and communication, it may be useful to emphasize a limited number of roles that are alluded to in theology and worship, but I see no good reason why three is always the right number.[18]

Understanding the Trinity as a way of pointing to the multiple roles of God and the varied way he relates to us provides a simple, straightforward understanding of one of the things the Trinity is trying to express. But differentiation is only one theme; unity and solidarity are another.

The Eastern branches of Christianity—Greek Orthodox, Russian Orthodox, Syriac Orthodox, etc.—have historically emphasized the differences between the "persons" of the Trinity more than the Western churches. Perhaps more accurately, they start with three persons and look for ways to express their unity. Among other things, this has the advantage of not reducing God to a super-powerful, human-like individual. This "individualistic god" probably contributed to the hyper-individualism of modern Western culture. Modern theologians such as Jürgen Moltmann and Miroslav Volf have developed the notion of the "social Trinity." They emphasize loving relationships the three persons have with one another. This still leaves the persons of the Trinity as the fundamental units. In general, it is difficult to imagine relationships without first imagining the identity of some units that are to be linked.

A more sociological approach may clarify some of these concepts. Western culture tends to think of individuals as the "real" elemental units out of which groups are formed. According to this

---

18. I see no strong theological reason—other than tradition—that God is experienced in three forms. There may be sociological reasons why there is a tendency toward emphasizing three actors. Most forms of dominance and conflict resolution require a minimum of three actors. Two actors can easily result in a standoff. Even the most physically and social dominant actor needs to sleep and hence is vulnerable. An alliance with a third actor provides a more stable and secure form of power. Similarly, three is the minimum number for people to express genuine social concern. Romantic couples and even good friends may care for one another because the care is reciprocated. True concern for others is shown when a third person requires sacrifices of the other two. My argument is not that "threeness" is inevitable, but that there may be structural pressures that encourage that outcome.

perspective, groups are "only" clusters of individuals. Historically and sociologically, this is empirically wrong.[19] Groups are at least as real as individuals. Without groups there would be no languages and no culture passed from one generation to the next—and hence no *human* beings. No human baby would survive without being the member of a group. Without groups there would be no individuals. Groups are literally the foundation of our being humans.[20]

Thinking of God as a group only becomes tritheism if we persist in the thinking of a group as only a collection of individuals. By drawing both on the notions of *social roles* and the *realness of social groups*, contemporary people can better grasp the core point of the Trinity: that there is one God who humans experience and relate to in multiple ways.

I am proposing a (somewhat) new pair of metaphors for understanding the Trinity. On the one hand, the three persons are analogous to the different social roles an individual plays in their day-to-day lives. On the other hand, we can think of the unity of three distinct persons as analogous to a "perfect version" of the solidarity of a loving group—keeping in mind that groups are just as real as individuals. The first metaphor starts with unity and moves to difference. The second starts with difference and moves to unity. I am not suggesting that all other metaphors should be discarded, but that these may be more comprehensible to contemporary people than many of the traditional theological discussions.

Though these sociological concepts provide a useful analogy for thinking about the relationship between the different ways of experiencing God, they say nothing specific about the content of these different aspects of God. The traditional persons of the Trinity are Father, Son, and Holy Ghost. As the word "ghost" became more associated with a threatening or scary being, "Holy Ghost"

---

19. Philosophers would probably see this as a case of "misplaced concreteness."

20. Of course, in more complex societies there are subgroups which may be largely a collection of individuals (e.g., all the first-year students at a large university or the "members" of Amazon's Prime service). None of these, however, could exist or operate did they not draw upon the "realness" of the broader group and culture.

SOME CLASSICAL DOCTRINES IN A NEW LANGUAGE

tended to be changed to "Holy Spirit." As feminism emerged, people became aware of the gender bias that was built into the limiting of God to male terms. Various churches have experimented with alternative formulations, with the most common alternative being "Creator, Redeemer, and Sustainer." But as critics have pointed out, the traditional terms referred to "persons" as actors, while these new terms refer to different functions. This suggests that the Father has no role as redeemer and creator, the Son has no role as a creator and sustainer, and the Holy Spirit has no connection to creation or redemption.

My own guess is that at least many parts of the church will eventually use an array of images to talk about the different ways that devotees experience God. In addition to saying, "Father, Son, and Holy Spirit," we might also say, "Divine Mother, Redeeming Daughter, and Holy Enchantress," or "Wondrous Parents, Awesome Sibling, and Holy Cheerleader." As the above phrases suggest, we need not totally abandon Trinitarian ideas. Neither should we limit ourselves to such triads. Ways in which we have experienced God may have no necessary parallel with the Trinity. Some examples might include: Awesome Creator, Reliable Guide, Supportive Companion, Inspiring Teacher, Holy Healer, Forgiving Judge, Loving Disciplinarian and Steadfast Sustainer.

I realize how awkward and weird these suggestions sound; hopefully others can come up with better terms. We must remember, however, that linguistic innovations often seem strange, but become taken for granted relatively quickly. In only a few years, the academic world shifted from "chairman" to "chairperson" or "chair." In the entertainment world, professionals rather quickly redefined the word "actor" so that it included women and men. "Gay" most commonly refers to a male homosexual instead of someone who is "joyful." Originally, "awful" did not imply "dreadful" or "terrible," but "full of awe." "Awesome" meant "profoundly reverential," but has become an overused cliché for enthusiastic approval of quite trivial matters.[21]

---

21. I am aware that to say a word originally meant A and now means B is a gross oversimplification of what is usually a complex etymological history.

UNDERSTANDING THE SACRED

The key point is that we can experience God in many forms and many ways. Hence, we need what I have called a multidimensional concept of God. The Trinity is a fourth-century attempt to express this. In the twenty-first century we probably need multiple ways of referring to the Trinity—remembering that human language will never be fully adequate to describe the wholly other and holy God.

A final sociological point: different groups of people are likely to find different terms or phrases meaningful. Teenagers talk differently than their parents and teachers; most minority groups have their own idioms; most professional groups create their own jargon. This does not mean anything goes. We should not, however, be immediately dismissive of the way other social groups express their understanding of God. This issue will be discussed more extensively in the section on religious pluralism.

You are probably tired of discussing abstract doctrines that focus on human faults or divine attributes. Such discussions are most helpful when taken in small doses. Hence, we will shift our focus to the worldly side of the Christian faith: the church.

My purpose here is not linguistic accuracy, but to stress that we often forget how language changes overtime and that such changes are often resented and contested.

Chapter 5

The Church

MOST MODERNS ARE UNAWARE of and uninterested in the doctrines and cults of the Egyptian Middle Kingdom. For doctrines to be of interest, they usually have to be part of an ongoing organization that impinges upon peoples' lives. For Christians this organization is the church. Hence, before discussing other doctrines we will turn to the nature and role of the church.

The Church as a "Turn-Off"

There seem to be three reasons so many people have abandoned "mainline" churches. The first is the primary focus of this book: theological language and concepts that seem nonsensical or bizarre to modern educated people. The second is the all-too-human social organization which is the chief proponent of Christianity, the church. People see church members engaged in hypocrisy, conflict, pettiness, and even meanness, not only in their secular lives, but also within the life of the church itself. They might expect this in places of employment, political parties, business and professional associations; this is the way such institutions are able to tolerate a significant amount of such behavior in order to accomplish the broader goals of the organization. Such behavior within an organization that is supposedly devoted to overcoming such tendencies seems especially offensive and phony. A third reason is that church members are often seen to be highly judgmental of others. In recent years such negative judgments have often been expressed about gender issues, sexuality, abortion, and end of life decisions—and a willingness of some more conservative Christians to create laws that enforce their views on others. Other Christians and churches that reject such intolerance are nonetheless looked upon with suspicion by secular members of the society. These are some of the reasons that many people distance themselves from the church. Many proclaim that they are "spiritual but not religious." So, for a theology that is trying to speak to people in a highly secularized culture, the doctrine of the church is not a peripheral matter.

The Centrality of Jesus

Organizations are usually stronger and more successful if they have a central and primary purpose, and if they have a visible leader who has some charisma. Microsoft's Bill Gates and Apple's Steve Jobs are the most obvious examples in the early decades of the twenty-first century. This is usually the case for religious movements too, and Jesus clearly played this role for the group of disciples and followers that eventually became the Christian church. Even today, the commonality of Christian churches is that they see Jesus Christ as the inspiration for their existence. They may vary greatly in their understanding of what "Jesus Christ" means and what is the most appropriate way to recognize his centrality. The classical formulation has been "Jesus is Lord." Whatever imagery or metaphor churches may adopt, proclaiming Christ centrality is the core criterion of a Christian church.

From a sociological point of view, Jesus was a charismatic leader. "Charisma" has come to refer to two clusters of meanings: (1) a personal attractiveness that inspires devotion in others and (2) a divinely given power or talent. Jesus as portrayed in the biblical texts is certainly a clear example of such a charismatic leader.

He affected people through his teachings, even if these sometimes puzzled or offended them. He also influenced people by his actions. Some were portrayed as miraculous, e.g., water into wine, walking on water, healing the lame and sick. Others were more mundane, e.g., washing the disciples' feet, seeking out and eating with those who were lowly and outcasts. In addition to specific words and actions, he influenced people with his passion, that is, his commitment to his calling—even though he knew such faithfulness would lead to his death on a cross. All of this repeatedly amazed people and gave the lowly new hope and vitality. Most extraordinary, his disciples experienced what was called "the resurrection." Whatever the factual details of what happened after Jesus's death, the early church experienced something extraordinary. They described these experiences as the resurrection and this was a crucial source of the new hope and energy of the early church.

The centrality of Jesus does not mean that he is the only manifestation of the Holy. The above discussion of the Trinity acknowledges that there are other ways of experiencing the Divine. Nonetheless, Jesus is the distinctive manifestation of God for those in the Christian church.

From Extraordinary to Ordinary

And it certainly was and is no good undertaking to reverse the sequences where by event precedes institution . . .

—Karl Barth[1]

The New Testament tells us two things: the church is centered on Jesus, who is extraordinary, but it is comprised of people who are very ordinary. Initially, its members were fishermen from Nazareth. The first disciples were "nobodies" from "Nowheresville." "Can anything good come out of Nazareth!?" (John 7:46). These lowly people took up the task of spreading the news about Jesus's teachings, actions, crucifixion, and resurrection. Before long, they were joined by more educated folk like Paul. But as Paul himself proclaims, he and the other early church leaders were not Jesus. While Jesus was extraordinary, his followers had to use more ordinary means to both remember and perpetuate the spirit of their extraordinary leader.

---

1. Barth, *Humanity of God*, 63 (emphsasis original).

This is a process that the famous German sociologist, Max Weber (1884–1920), called the "routinization of charisma." There have been many charismatic leaders. Eventually, the charismatic leader dies or disappears from the empirical, historical world. If the leader's teachings, actions, and inspiration are not to fade away, these must be converted into routines that more ordinary people can sustain over time. Teachings and experiences must be standardized and written down (or memorized); regular meetings must be arranged; a place for meetings must be found; some individuals must prepare and lead these meetings. New generations must be taught about the founder and what happened. If the movement is to spread, newcomers must be recruited and educated. In the process of doing this, even well-intended people often disagree. What exactly did the founder say and do? What is the best way to memorialize the founder? Often there are disagreements and fights over how to select the leader of this more routinized structure.

To say it another way, an ongoing tension between the *otherness of the sacred* and the *ordinariness of profane routines*. Often the profane routines become sacred. We see this in bureaucracies when filling out the forms displaces the goal of serving clients. We see it in churches when rituals are more sacred than Jesus's command that we love one another—and the struggle for social justice that this implies. This tug of war to balance the relationship between the sacred and profane never ends.

Why Join a Church: The Bad News and the Good News

> *Private Christianity is not Christianity at all. Private theology is not free theology; it is not theology at all.*
>
> —KARL BARTH[2]

So, the person joining a church should not expect to find a community of people who are always "nice." Joining the church is more like joining Alcoholics Anonymous than joining a country

---

2. Barth, *Humanity of God*, 95.

club. (If a church is like a country club or a holier-than-thou society, stay clear of it.) An Alcoholics Anonymous group is a bunch of drunks trying to stay sober for another day; they recognize how weak they are alone and that they need the support of others—and the support of a higher power. The church is a group of people who recognize and confess that they are deeply flawed but have great potential for expressing lovingkindness. They deal with their faults by trying to do a bit better each day. Not only do they recognize the flaws of individuals, but they know that often they live in tragic circumstances: a troubled marriage, a handicapped child, a boring and demeaning job, a war zone. They realize that they cannot heal themselves or cope with their circumstances on their own. Not only do they need the support of the other flawed church members, but they also need the support of a higher power—and they have come to believe that Jesus Christ is the best expression of and link to such power.

The recognition that they are deeply flawed does not mean they have to become depressed hair shirts or sad sacks. Jesus's message was not that people were flawed and often trapped in very bad circumstances—this had long been recognized by the Hebrew Scriptures (and most of the other world religions). Rather, the good news (i.e., the gospel), is that Jesus Christ is a new source of healing and power. As noted above, the gospel comes through his teachings, actions, passion, and resurrection. Despite the church's many flaws, this healing and power are best experienced through life in a congregation.

Other techniques such as meditation can be carried out alone. These are self-help devices that may be useful, but they do not fully recognize that we are incapable of "saving ourselves." Salvation, like life in general, is a social endeavor.

This does not mean that joining the church or developing a relationship with Jesus will make everything okay or prevent failures and lapses. Rather, you become part of a community who each week renews their awareness of their failings, their call to seek justice and love, and their access to a transcendent source of power.

Of course, meditation can take place in an ongoing community that offers solace and interpersonal support. In general, however, meditation classes (not to speak of strictly personal meditation) are weak in offering prophetic criticism of social injustices. Nor does meditation per se usually offer the social support of a good congregation. Meditation may, however, be a key source of the courage and stamina to engage in such activities. In short, meditation is an important and useful tool, but not a substitute for regular collective worship.

Congregations: From Fans to Players

Much of the discussion above focuses on "the church." This concept recognizes that there is a type of reality beyond particular congregations. In some respects, this is similar to the way that baseball is a reality beyond any particular team or group of teams. It is legitimate to make generalizations about baseball, and it is legitimate to make statements about the church.

People can be baseball fans without ever having played baseball, but they will have a more existential sense of the game if they have been a member of a team and actually played the game. The attempt to be "spiritual, but not religious" is like being a fan, but not a player. You avoid dealing with concrete vices and virtues of other team members; you also avoid dealing with their perceptions of your vices and virtues. Jesus did not call upon people to be his fans; he called them to be his disciples. Christianity is a game for players. Collectively this means that a congregation is a team, not an audience. The difficulty in making this transition increases as the size of the congregation becomes larger. Too often large congregations, centered on a popular preacher, are more like an audience of fans than members of a committed team. This is not to condemn all large congregations; some are made up of players, but some are mainly audiences seeking entertainment and reassurance.

Ideally, a congregation is for all players: poor ones, great ones, consistent ones and erratic ones, losers and winners. As Paul famously said: "There is no longer Jew or Greek, there is no longer slave or free, there is no longer male and female; for all of you are one in Christ Jesus" (Galatians 3: 28). This is largely true for the church, but rarely is this so for any given congregation.

Some Are More Equal than Others

George Orwell's *Animal Farm* is an allegory criticizing Lenin and Stalin's Soviet Union. All the farm animals rebel against their exploiting human master and set up a supposedly utopian animal society. Before long, however, the pigs, which are the smartest animals, become the decision-makers. The dogs, which are the fiercest, become the enforcers. The pigs complain that making all the decisions is a heavy burden. This supposedly justifies an official order that all of the apples and milk should be delivered to the pigs—to ensure that the decision-makers are in good health. The original ideological motto, "All animals are equal," becomes, "All animals are equal, but some animals are *more equal than others.*"

For the church, the relationship between spiritual equality and inequality are the mirror image of *Animal Farm*—the inequalities involve not greater privileges, but greater levels of commitment. All are sinners and are loved equally by God. Yet, people vary in their understanding of their faith and their commitment to the work of the church. The new Christian must prepare to be one in Christ, not only with the saints, but also the lukewarm, the well-intended but inept, and the hypocrites. Even more disconcerting is that the same person can at times display more than one these characteristics.

On the other hand, most local congregations are often quite "equal" (i.e., homogeneous) with respect to language, ethnicity, socioeconomic status, and political inclinations. Even congregations dedicated to overcoming this tendency often have limited success. People can have religious commitments that they sincerely share with others who are quite different in their cultural background. Nonetheless carrying out the day-to-day task of a congregation is greatly simplified if people come from relatively similar backgrounds. Sharing appealing abstractions is easier than agreeing on concrete practices.

This does not mean we should give up in our efforts to seek social justice. Our failure to adequately accomplish this should not cause us to overlook another form of equality: we are all equal in the love we receive from God, in the availability of Jesus Christ, and in the power offered by the Holy Spirit. This is not a substitute for social justice, but it is a resource that can sustain and renew us in our efforts to transform the social and cultural worlds in which we live.

Pluralism

When I was in high school and college, denominational boundaries tended to be relatively strong and cooperation among local churches was the exception rather than the rule. At the national and international level, however, this was probably the height of the Ecumenical Movement. The World Council of Churches were formed in 1948. The National Council of Churches of Christ in the U.S.A. came into being in 1950. The British Council of Churches was formed in 1942 and eventually became the Churches Together in Britain and Ireland. The Conference of European Churches was formed in 1959.

In my last two years in college I was chair of a committee that organized an annual regional ecumenical conference that included students and clergy from a variety of denominations. Though virtually all colleges and schools in our area—Texas and surrounding states—were racially segregated, students and clergy from several African-American colleges attended these conferences. At that time, I had hopes that this might eventually take the form of a "united church" in which denominational organizations would merge—demonstrating that at least organizationally "we are all one in Christ." I no longer think this is possible or desirable.

In the earlier section entitled "The Nature of Status..." I pointed out that as status systems become larger they tend to fragment and become more pluralistic and develop multiple subcultures.

The inexpansibility of status contributes to this tendency. In a large system, any given individual is likely to be less visible, have less status, and have less contact with those who have high status. Empirical research suggests this tendency applies to churches: the larger the denomination, the more likely are schisms.[3]

Having lived overseas seven times and in several large metropolitan areas, I am aware of the variety of cultural backgrounds and emotional needs that people have. I doubt that an ardently Pentecostal congregation or a very traditional Roman Catholic parish would be spiritually satisfying for me. I can, however, see how other people might be attracted to such churches.

Hence, pluralism per se is not a vice, but a virtue. What is a vice is an arrogant certainty that there is only one legitimate way to develop a relationship with Jesus, to receive God's grace, and to experience the power of the Holy Spirit.

Pluralism does not mean that any group that calls itself Christian is legitimate. The Klu Klux Klan was supposedly "Christian," yet it committed numerous lynchings and other forms of intimidation—and re-emerged in 2017 as a defender of White privilege. In north Guyana, Jonestown claimed to be a American Christian community, yet in 1978 on the orders of their leader there were several murders and the mass suicide of over nine hundred people.

Nor is pluralism easy. In my opinion, liberals are often overly optimistic about the prospect of creating pluralistic societies. If we have great difficulty accomplishing this in most congregations and most metropolitan areas, success at the macro-societal level is likely to be even more difficult.[4]

---

3. Liebman et al., "Exploring ... Sources of Denominationalism," 343–52.

4. This is especially the case if the pluralism comes about because elites want to recruit immigrants for cheap labor but not pay the fringe benefits and taxes that are required to successfully integrate these groups into the host society. The theological point is that however good the intentions may be, peace and justice will not be accomplished by churches serving as temporary sponsors and being opposed to all restrictions on immigration—though these may be legitimate in some contexts. Of course, the opposite is also true: the solution is not building walls or demonizing immigrants.

Not just tolerance, but openness should be our approach to developing relationships with non-Christian religious groups from other parts of the world. Criticizing certain practices of other religious traditions may very well be appropriate, for example, degrading behavior toward women, or the use of inherited social categories to privilege some and degrade others. But at the same time, we should listen carefully to the criticisms that they might have of Christian beliefs and practices.

As members of a particular congregation and of the greater church, we must avoid naiveté. Nonetheless, the default assumption in our relationship with both Christian and non-Christian groups should be one of openness, tolerance, cooperation, and love, realizing that we cannot attain these without God's grace.

The Church and the World

Certainly, the church has a role in helping people to deal with things that cannot be changed. We all die, most of us will lose loved ones, and some of us will have spouses or children who become criminals or addicts. So, the church has an important pastoral role in helping members deal with human finitude and the sins of individuals. The church also has an important priestly role in helping people relate to the Divine. More will be said about this when we consider worship.

Equally important is the church's role in legitimizing or transforming the everyday profane world. We must remember that the main vision Jesus proclaimed was a collective one: the commonwealth of God. Different Christians have had varying understandings of how the church should relate to the profane world. Here I can only briefly survey some of the alternatives and state what I see to be the most viable strategies for relatively well-educated moderns.[5]

---

5. For a similar but more elaborate discussion of alternative forms churches and more generally Christianity might take, see Long, *Nature and Future of Christianity*.

First, we need to acknowledge that through much of history the chief effect of the church on the broader world was to sanctify the status quo. Frequently, the church provided an *ideology that hid or legitimated injustice*—including the exploitation of the more vulnerable and less powerful. A second and very different strategy is for the church to be an alternative community that serves as a *beacon of what is possible*. Many such communities were pacifists. The moral compromises of conventional worldly patterns—which most of us follow—are made more evident by their witness. Such communities tended to physically isolate themselves from the profane world, and often to rely on established political authorities for protection. Consequently, the effect of their witness is often limited. A third perspective sees church as a *leaven* that quietly tries to make the world a better place; perhaps this is the most common pattern in the contemporary developed world. A fourth alternative is the church as a *prophetic critic*. Only a few congregations define themselves in this way and they usually have difficulty sustaining themselves over multiple generations. The wider church, however, has been pretty consistent in producing prophetic individuals who have supportive followers. Their criticism can be aimed at the injustices of existing economic and political structures or at the failure of the church to speak out against these. A fifth role of the church may be *offering hope* in seemingly hopeless situations such as natural disasters, civil wars, and plagues.

A sixth way of relating to the world is a combination of the second and third visions: the church as a *good neighbor*. Probably Jesus's most famous of parable is the story of the Good Samaritan (Luke 10:25–37), in which a member of a hated group shows what neighborliness means. But in an enormous, complex, globalized, urbanized world, we come into contact with many people who need help whom we do not consider neighbors in any concrete sense. The modern form of neighborliness cannot be limited to those with whom we meet face to face but must include multitudes of people we do not know. Usually, they must be helped via complex bureaucracies. This is one reason the church should be concerned about social policies and programs and the political processes that shape these. The concept that is now commonly used to legitimate assistance to the vulnerable is "human rights." This fundamental notion is that people have a right not to be persecuted. I may also include a right to health care, education, and minimum levels of income. The theological and political problem is that this stress on rights shifts the emphasis from the generosity of the Good Samaritan to the demands of those who need help. The implicit demands in the language of "rights" often create resistance and resentment. Rights need to be linked to responsibilities. This emphasis on responsibilities, however, often ignores that privileged elites usually get to define "rights" and "responsibilities." Moreover, the costs of new rights for the underprivileged usually fall upon those who are only slightly better off. "Rights" and "responsibilities" may be one way to decrease injustice, but seldom do they match the generosity of true neighbors as exemplified by the Good Samaritan.

These six ways of relating to the profane world are certainly not an exhaustive list. Nor or these categories mutually exclusive. All except the first approach—justifying injustice—are legitimate ways for groups of Christians to express their faith. The temptation of most congregations is to engage in *ministries of mercy*—food and clothing for the poor—and to neglect or avoid *ministries of justice*. Advocating fair housing laws, opposing job discrimination, and protesting police misconduct can all create great controversy. Ministries of mercy are legitimate, but we need to remember that Jesus was not killed because he fed the hungry or healed the sick; he was crucified because he criticized the religious leaders of his day and was seen as a threat to economic and political establishment. If we are to be his true disciples, we will probably make someone mad, and we need to be prepared to deal with their hostility. Jesus did not seek crucifixion, and neither should we. But we should not expect membership in the church to be cheap and we should realize that true discipleship can be extremely costly.

Now let us return to the task of trying to make the church more attractive to people by better articulating some additional classical doctrines.

Chapter 6

More Doctrines in a New Language

Providence

The way this happens is identical with the Divine mystery and beyond calculation or description.

—Paul Tillich[1]

How does God intervene in human affairs? Traditionally this is referred to as God's providence. The term "providence" has largely fallen out of fashion in contemporary religious discussion. The *Oxford English Dictionary* gives a number of definitions of providence, but in the context of theology these are the two that are most relevant: "The foreknowing and protective care of God (or nature, etc.); divine direction, control, or guidance," and "an act or instance of divine intervention; an event or circumstance which indicates divine dispensation." The article on "Providence" in the *Oxford Handbook of Systematic Theology* defines this key concept as: "How, if at all, God is involved in what happens in the course of our lives day to day, in the course of human history, and in the 'natural history' of the world around us."[2] More concretely, what role did God play in the recent bountiful harvest, peace and disarmament treaties, and medical advances, as well as the earthquakes, tsunamis, airline crashes, civil wars, and children dying of cancer?

Does God intervene in nature, in history, and in our personal lives? If so, how does this occur? The first thing that needs to be

---

1. Tillich, *Systematic Theology*, 3:373.
2. Wood, *Oxford Handbook of Systematic Theology*, 91.

said is that no one can answer such questions with certainty. The concept of providence does not negate the centrality of mystery. Nonetheless from what we know now, God seldom (if ever) intervenes in natural physical processes. To say that God uses natural events to punish the wicked but shields the righteous is, at best, empirically dubious and theologically dangerous. This presumes we know with certainty what individuals and groups are godly. Otherwise the argument becomes circular: these terrible things happened to them because they engaged in evil; we know they engaged in evil because God brought disaster upon them. At least some interpretations of the Old Testament figure Job see him as rightly protesting against such ideas centuries ago. (Why a loving God allows such destructive events at all is a question I will deal with when I discuss the problem of evil.)

But people are affected by more than physical processes. They are strongly shaped by the social relationships they have with others and the experiences they share. The joy of a wedding or the pain of a loved one's death does not occur primarily through physical mechanism, but through the impact of symbols on our emotions. Of course, our emotions operate through physical processes, but symbols usually trigger these processes. The words communicated by a letter or voiced through airwaves can bring either joy or sadness. The very same message may cause some to rejoice and others to grieve. That is, we can be much affected by the content of symbolic communication.

Therefore, one obvious way that we can think about Divine intervention in human events is through humans' communication with God and other devotees. Such communications are analogous to what occurs in social relationships. Communication with God typically happens through prayer, worship, song, meditation, and sacred scriptures. These can impact devotees' own actions in both sacred and profane activities. This includes the way people react to physical phenomena: awe at the beauty and power of nature, joy and thanksgiving for a newborn, or the anxiety and dread of a diagnosis of cancer.

MORE DOCTRINES IN A NEW LANGUAGE

But communication and relationship with the Sacred One, the Holy Other, is not easy. To use a human parallel, we may feel like we are trying to communicate with someone from a different culture who speaks a different language. An infinite difference in status further complicates communication. If we are trying to connect with a very high-status person we often fear being ignored, rejected, or misunderstood. The problem is lessened if we are introduced by someone who knows both of us and speaks both of our languages, that is, an interpreter, mediator, or intercessor. Communication between humans and gods seems to be aided by the deity taking the form of humans. The Holy Other becomes more accessible and the relationship more intimate. This is one reason that gods incarnated as humans are found in a number of religions. Obviously, Jesus as the incarnation of God is a central Christian doctrine. We do not have to believe in a literal virgin birth or bodily resurrection to appreciate the significance of Jesus in helping us to understand God.

Language is the kind of communication that makes us human, but this is not our only medium of communication. Art, music, gestures, facial expressions, meditation, and rituals are additional ways of connecting with others. These are especially significant because they tend to create shared emotions. Events as diverse as individual meditation, a military parade or a religious worship service can impact people's emotions. Many people in social situations feel affected or "moved by" an "external force." Emile Durkheim, the French sociologist mentioned in chapter 2, referred to this as "collective effervescence." The concept refers to a shared emotional state that emerges in groups of people who have a common focus and share in similar rituals. This is at least one way to think of the Holy Spirit. According to the biblical tradition, the Holy Spirit is a primary way that God intervenes in the mundane events of everyday life.

The above discussion suggests ways we can think of God's providential interventions in our individual and collective lives without seeing these as magic or miracles. This understanding of Providence does not eliminate the role of human action. Nor does it deny the possibility of historical contingency: simply having the bad luck of being in the wrong place at the wrong time—or the good luck of being at the right place at the right time.[3]

On the other hand, I see no need to assert that God's interventions are necessarily restricted to the ways scientists and other scholars currently understand the natural and social world. Certainly, things happen that we do not understand. Of course, we should support science and scholarship that provides various kinds of explanations to some of these mysteries, but we should also seek a level of humility that recognizes both the value and the limitations of such cognitive accomplishments. Mystery is, and will continue to be, part of the human experience, and we need ways to embrace this fact. As William Cowper's famous hymn says, "God moves in a mysterious way; His wonders to perform."[4]

Revelation

How do we know God? This is often answered in terms of the idea of revelation. In most cultures, during most periods of history, "the slings and arrows of outrageous fortune"—to use Hamlet's famous line—have driven people to seek alliances with more powerful beings. But humans seeking gods is not enough. Gods must reveal themselves—or at least humans must be convinced that they have. In this sense, revelation is a special case of providence; it focuses on a particular way that God intervenes in the human world.

Again, an analogy with social relationships is useful. For anyone to have social status, they must be socially visible. They must not hide. Usually they must work at making themselves visible. The guy with the beautiful voice who sings only in the shower is not likely to become a famous opera star.

Similarly, for anything to be sacred, it must be visible to potential devotees. Gods must (1) reveal themselves, (2) devotees must be paying attention and looking in the "right direction," and

---

3. In this context "right" and "wrong" are not used in a moral sense but refer to whether the outcome is beneficial or harmful.

4. Cowper, *Light Shining out of Darkness*.

(3) an intimate relationship between them needs to emerge and be sustained over time. Many theological discussions have drawn a distinction between general revelation and special revelation. The first of these refers to knowledge of God that comes through natural means: awe at the vastness of the cosmos or natural beauty, the use of rational thought, the behavior of saintly humans. Special revelation refers to instances when God deliberately and more directly makes herself visible to humans. Sacred scriptures and events that are believed to be miracles are the most common form of special revelation across a variety of religious communities. For Christians, the signature events are the life, death, and resurrection of Jesus. Some famous theologians, for example Karl Barth, would argue that knowledge of the true God is only available through Jesus Christ and the Bible, and that all other attempts to know God are, at best, misguided. I believe such a claim is both unnecessary and arrogant. The alternative is not to accept the opposite claim that all religions are essentially the same and of equal value.

Knowing someone well is not a momentary event; people change and one's knowledge of another must be repeatedly updated. Marriages and friendships are ongoing relationships that require continuing efforts to sustain. Nor can they be sustained solely by the private efforts of one or even both of the partners. Most marriages are sustained in part by networks of relatives and friends who, often unconsciously, create social pressure for the marriage to be sustained. Private meditation and prayer may be useful, but they are not an adequate substitute for regular collective worship. This is the reason that periodic public worship is so central to most religious traditions—a matter I will take up below.

While analogies with human relationships are useful, we must always remember that God-human relationships are different from human-human ones in important ways. This is one reason why the Trinity has continued to be important. The doctrine recognizes that God has multiple aspects, some of which are not analogous to social relationships—and that such analogies can be dangerous. This is the important insight of Islam, which rejects all images of God, and especially those that portray God as a human-like figure. But good theology, like much of life, is a matter of steering between competing values, dangers, and temptations. Being too preoccupied with avoiding one danger can lead to becoming deformed by another. On the whole, I think that drawing on our knowledge of human relationships in order to know God is useful—and probably inevitable.

Like human relationships, our relationship with God changes over time because new insights are revealed to us. Moreover, at least some things we thought we knew about God are revealed to be less important than we originally believed. Reading and studying the Bible is an essential form of revelation, but historically, our understanding of many of these texts has evolved. The same is true of other forms of revelation. Hence, revelation, the way God reveals herself and our knowledge of God is not fixed for all time but is in process.

Salvation

> *This much is certain, that we have no theological right to set any sort of limits to the loving-kindness of God which has appeared in Jesus Christ. Our theological duty is to see and understand it as being still greater than we had seen before.*
>
> —Karl Barth[5]

Salvation usually refers to the state of being saved from sin or evil, and hence having a right relationship with God. Salvation may or may not refer to actually entering into bliss or some kind of utopian afterlife. Here I will deal with three key concepts that are associated with salvation: grace, atonement, and eschatology.

---

5. Barth, *Humanity of God*, 62.

MORE DOCTRINES IN A NEW LANGUAGE

Law versus Grace

A seemingly perpetual controversy of Christian theology concerns how humans attain salvation—and more specifically, the relative importance of law and grace, of human works or God's works. In Christian theology, grace refers to an unmerited gift. Jesus criticized the Pharisees for following the minutiae of religious rules and ignoring their spirit and intent. Galatians, one of the earliest books of the New Testament, records a theological controversy between Paul and Peter over whether Gentile Christians had to conform to the Jewish law. Saint Augustine of Hippo (354–430) debated a version of this issue with the British ascetic and monk Pelagius (c. 360–418). Whatever Pelagius's actual views—and this is debated—Pelagianism came to mean that humans have free will and the capacity to earn salvation by their own efforts; for Augustine, humans were so deeply corrupted by sin that only God's forgiveness and grace could provide salvation. Martin Luther (1483–1546) debated with the papacy over the legitimacy of indulgences (i.e., making contributions to the church to shorten a soul's time in purgatory). Luther condemned such practices and emphasized salvation occurred through faith alone. He rejected any notion that humans could bargain with God or buy her favor—rather than receive it as a gracious, unmerited gift. There have been numerous variations of this issue over the course of the church's history—and similar debates in other religious traditions.

Drawing on sociological terms, salvation can be thought of as the ultimate form of *status transformation* and *upward mobility* available to humans. I do not mean, of course, that salvation is becoming richer and more powerful in a worldly sense. Rather, our familiarity with social mobility can serve as a useful metaphor or analogy. Then we can ask how people acquire status. This can help us to better understand the source and means of salvation. As indicated in chapter two, there are two key sources of status: *conformity* to the norms of the group and social *associations*.

In nearly all Christian theology, salvation comes about not by conformity to rules, but through an intimate association with

God.[6] This is analogous to the effect of your intimate social associations on your own personality. This is recognized in the Bible: "Whoever walks with the wise becomes wise, but the companion of fools suffers harm" (Proverbs 13:20).[7] The reverse can also be true. Saintly people are often able to transform the fools into the wise, the self-centered into the loving, and the banal into the extraordinary. For Christians, association with Jesus Christ, whose sacredness is beyond saintliness, is the primary means of bringing about such transformations.

Prayer and worship are relevant in most religious traditions as a means of developing an intimate association with gods. But Jesus Christ changes the possibilities of such association with God. His example of his own relationship with God as Abba provides a model to follow. Many people more easily relate to a god in human form than to a divinity who is abstract or amorphous. Jesus, the Christ, serves as the mediator between the "totally other" God, and finite human beings. Associating with God via Jesus Christ is not, however, primarily a way to live up to God's laws or expectations; rather, these are ways of becoming open to God. The association with the Divine shapes our subsequent behavior and who we are. It accomplishes this by reforming and transforming our social and personal identity in this life. This acceptance and transformation is never complete; we are still sinful human beings who fail to live up to our

---

6. While most theology emphasizes grace over works, the behavior of Christians and the policies of the church have not always reflected this. Even within theological writings there are a whole series of "subdebates" over whether humans have the free will to accept or reject such grace or whether it is "irresistible"—and hence salvation is due solely to the gracious acts of God. Another variety of this issue is the relation between nature and grace. The Catholic tradition sees humans as corrupted by sin, but human nature still has some residue of goodness that can be expanded by grace. Calvinist and Lutheran traditions see human nature as totally corrupted; it can be redeemed solely by God's grace. These matters are often a key theological difference between different branches of the church. These debates parallel the debates in the social sciences over the degree to which behavior is a matter of human agency and choice or primarily shaped by historically antecedent social and cultural structures.

7. There are other similar passages in the Hebrew Bible. For a New Testament example, see 1 Corinthians 15:33.

own standards, not to speak of God's. Nonetheless, the core meaning of Christian salvation is being healed, restored, and reconciled by an intimate, transforming relationship with Jesus.

One temptation is to affirm that association is the means of salvation in principle, but in day-to-day behavior we concentrate on enforcing rules and conformity—especially on other people. The other temptation is antinomianism, the idea that because one is saved by the gospel of grace via association with Jesus, conformity to the moral law is of no use or obligation; no rules apply.

As mentioned above, there are differences in human associations and divine ones. High-status humans have limited time and energy; even the most generous celebrity or saint cannot provide a transforming intimacy to everyone. God can. Humans—even saints—can get fed up with the failures and unfaithfulness of others and end relationships. God does not. She is always available to those who seek her presence—even if we are unable to sense this presence.

Much more could and has been said about the nature of salvation. The earliest New Testament texts deal with how salvation is brought about. This continues to be a central concern of nearly all varieties of theology. Drawing the parallels between salvation and upward status transformation *is only one useful metaphor*—and like all metaphors this one fails to capture the full reality to which it refers. It is, however, more understandable to contemporary people than many traditional concepts.

As indicated above, the salvation that Jesus proclaimed involved not just the transformation of individuals, but of the broader society and world. People's ability to accept Divine grace and restore a right relationship with God is affected by whether the people they associate with have also experienced such redemption. As noted above, a concrete social example of this is found in what are often called twelve-step groups such as Alcoholics Anonymous. Many of these groups explicitly recognized that both social support and the help of some transcendent power are needed. Such support of both God and other Christians is the core significance of the church, and a key reason why Christians must be concerned with creating a just and caring society.

How are God's love and gracious efforts to save and redeem—via an intimate relationship with Jesus Christ—to be reconciled with Gods demands for justice? One way of addressing this question has been the doctrine of atonement.

Atonement and Reconciliation

There is no one, tidy theory of the atonement to be plucked either from the New Testament or the wider tradition.

—RUPERT SHORT[8]

According to the *Merriam-Webster Dictionary* to "atone" means "to supply satisfaction, [to] expiate; to make amends [as in] atone for sins." Atonement has long been associated with various forms of sacrifice. Other religions have also had varying understandings of sacrifice. Hence a brief review of some of these alternates is appropriate to better understand the Christian notion of atonement.

A Note on Sacrifice

. . . my mother brought to certain oratories, erected in the memory of the saints, offerings of porridge, bread, and wine—as had been her custom in Africa—and she was forbidden to do so by the doorkeeper . . . And as soon as she learned that it was the bishop who had forbidden it, she acquiesced . . . devoutly and obediently. . .

—AUGUSTINE OF HIPPO[9]

There are many kinds of prayer: prayers of praise, of petition, of thanksgiving, for forgiveness, for courage and strength, etc.

---

8. Shortt, "Slave in Your Place," 42–43.
9. Augustine of Hippo, *Confessions*, 81.

Similarly, religious sacrifices are conducted for a variety of reasons: thanksgiving, praising, warding off evil or disaster, and atoning for sins, etc. Hence, sacrifice is not necessarily link to the notion of atonement, but this is probably the most common rationale within the Christian tradition.

Exactly what kinds of sacrifice are appropriate and the meaning of these sacrifices have long been controversial in many religions including Christianity. Nonetheless, many types of sacrifices are intended to accomplish a form of *status transformation*, or more precisely *status restoration*. The sins and shortcomings of humans can be placed upon a sacrificial victim. The victim is a substitute for the humans.[10] With this interpretation of sacrifice, the intent is to shift the sins and impurities of the one who provides the sacrificial offering onto the items being offered for sacrifice. These items are "destroyed"—for example, killing a sacrificial animal, or breaking a loaf of bread. The destruction of the now-impure offering restores the spiritual status of the one who supplies the offering. This is the key imagery behind what are called *substitutionary doctrines of the atonement*, in which Jesus is the sacrificial victim that is substituted for humankind to atone for their sin. The assumption is that this makes human sinners more acceptable to God; intimacy with God is restored. This is often linked with the notion of sharing some portion of what has been "destroyed"—often this involves sharing food with God. Such intimacy with the deity restores the status of the worshiper. In the Christian tradition, this takes the form of the Eucharist or Lord's Supper. sharing of the broken bread, which is the symbol for Christ's body, and the sharing the wine, which is the symbol for Christ's spilt blood.[11]

This substitutionary doctrine of the atonement has become an "orthodox" teaching for many branches of the church.

---

10. This may involve repressed anger and redirected violence, but this is not necessarily the case. See Girard et al., *Violence and the Sacred*.

11. Traditions within Christianity have differed over whether the bread and the wine, which are the elements of the Eucharist, are symbols, or whether they are in some physical or spiritual sense transformed into the body and blood of Christ. Increasingly educated people tend to affirm the symbolic understanding of the Eucharist.

Scholars, however, debate whether this concept is found in the New Testament. The first formal statement of the doctrine is usually attributed to the British monk St. Anselm, and this did not occur until nearly a thousand years after the death of Jesus. Hence, a number of contemporary theologians have reconsidered the usefulness of this understanding of atonement and explored other ways of thinking about sacrifices.

The key point for contemporary theology is that sacrifice can have multiple meanings, both explicit and implicit meanings. The Eucharist, the central form of ritual sacrifice for most Christians, is probably most powerful when the logic and rationale for the sacrifice is left at least partially implicit.

Different groups with varying historical and personal experiences may well find that some images, sentiments, and rationales are more meaningful to them than others. For example, James Cone explains why Jesus's blood, and more generally his suffering, is so central to Black churches in the U.S.; Black Americans had experienced the violence of lynching and intimidation and could grasp the parallel with Jesus' crucifixion.[12]

But no matter how sacrifice is interpreted, the key goal can be to bring about atonement and reconciliation between God and her devotees, which in turn gives the devotees renewed strength and energy.

Other Forms of Reconciliation

Sacrifice is only one of the images used to represent reconciliation. The Old Testament scholar Walter Brueggemann, for example, suggests:

> ... we might see the crucifixion of Jesus the ultimate act of prophetic criticism in which Jesus announces the end of a world of death ... and takes death into his own person ... the ultimate criticism is not one of triumphant indignation but one of passion and compassion that

---

12. Cone, *Cross and the Lynching Tree*, 65–75.

completely and irresistibly undermine the work of competence and competition.[13]

This transforms the crucifixion into an act of prophetic resistance rather than priestly atonement.

American Baptist theologian Mark Heim criticizes substitutionary doctrine of the atonement and offers an alternative. As noted above, various forms of sacrifice are found in most societies. A subliminal intent of sacrifice was to build the solidarity needed for social life by sacrificing a victim who is "other" than the members of the community. Heim argues that the sacrifice of Jesus was not about renewing the established community by killing a victim, but about identifying with the victims who are sacrificed. Jesus death is a sacrifice to end such sacrifices and offer a new source of solidarity and peace.[14]

Others concepts of reconciliation include images of paying the owner of slaves for their freedom, penal images of the pardoning or releasing of criminals, legal images such as providing justifications for not imposing the usual penalties, medical images of healing and restoration of health, escape images as in the exodus of the Hebrews from Egyptian slavery, images of victory over sin and death—and this is not an exhaustive list.

The church has long used a variety of metaphors and analogies to understand how the relationship between humans and God is restored. Any one metaphor is inadequate. The key point is that despite our flaws and willful self-centeredness, and despite our obliviousness to the injustices of taken-for-granted ideologies and social patterns, God has acted to restore the human-Divine relationship. This helps to heal our physical and emotional wounds and to reinvigorate our commitment to social justice.

We need to remember that such concepts as grace and incarnation point to the fact that this human healing involves God's voluntary "downward mobility." This is a prerequisite to our own "upward mobility." As Barth says, "Without the condescension of

---

13. Brueggemann, *Prophetic Imagination*, 94–95.
14. Heim, *Saved from Sacrifice*.

God, there would be no exaltation of man."[15] What we can testify to is that some combination of these metaphors restores our relationship with God—and we experience this as a form of salvation in the present and the future.

Eschatology

Eschatology is the part of theology that discusses the end of human history, and often an anticipated afterlife. These have included images of an apocalyptic end of the world, the second coming of Christ, the raising of the dead, and a final judgment that will determine whether particular individuals will attain salvation. (Some fundamentalists and evangelicals use the term "rapture" to refer to the initiation of these final events.) The content of eschatological visions often involves a reversal of the worldly status structure. For example: "many who are first will be last and the last will be first" (Mathew 19:30). Why such reversals occur is by no means clear. Scholars, especially social scientists, usually assume that the eschatological visions are fantasies that make the injustices of the world more tolerable and hence reduce resistance to the established order. The usual assumption is that the worldly structure shapes the afterlife, which offers hope for the future and makes the present more tolerable: "blessed are the meek for they shall inherit the earth (Matthew 5:3). But the direction of causation may in some circumstances be the opposite; the vision of the next world, as well as other theological concepts, may shape the historical social structure. The Hindu doctrine of near-endless reincarnations—first a Brahmin, then an insect, then a peasant, then a king, etc.—may promote a caste-like social structure that values stability and predictability; hence, people cannot (publicly) change their caste during their lifetime. The possibility of a future beloved community may very well shape Christian's expectations about what is a legitimate social structure. In short,

---

15. Barth, *Humanity of God*, 48.

eschatological visions should not be "explained away" or dismissed as only misguided fantasies.[16]

A common Christian view of salvation is that after death people will continue to live in a more perfect place in intimate and loving relationship to God and one another. Some see this happening immediately after death while others think this will not happens until the end history and the raising of the dead.

Theoretical physics suggests that multiple realms of reality are a possibility, but there is no empirical evidence for this. Hence, while I am doubtful that there is an afterlife, I think it is unwise and unnecessary to absolutely reject a notion of heaven or paradise. But neither should we take for granted that such a place literally exists or that traditional ideas about salvation, such as heaven or hell, are accurate. Rather, when I refer to salvation, I mean such notions as redemption, regeneration, reconciliation, liberation, escape, deliverance, that is, an overcoming of our human frailties and our alienation from one another and God—whether in this or some future life.[17] I see no basis or need for trying to specify what this would mean in more concrete or literal terms. Even in earlier centuries, images of the afterlife were articulated by literary metaphor and analogy rather than accounts that claimed to be empirically accurate. Dante Alighieri's *Divine Comedy*, Paul Bunyan's *Pilgrim's Progress*, and John Milton's *Paradise Lost* are classic examples of such efforts.

But the biblical understanding of salvation is not primarily about the future of a given individual. Rather, Jesus proclaims the coming of the commonwealth of God. That is, salvation will involve a transformation the existing creation, including social and political order, resulting in a new "heaven" and a new "earth."[18]

---

16. Milner, *Hindu Eschatology*; and Milner, *Status and Sacredness*, 204–25. This tendency toward reversal seems to be a sociological process that affects the theology of a number of religious traditions, but I cannot deal with this issue here.

17. For a discussion of the problems that various terms might entail see Tillich, *Systematic Theology*, 3:168–72.

18. Multiple references in the Bible suggest a transformation of existence, not simply of some selected/elected individuals or the emergence of a particular

In short, we need to remain extremely modest in what we assert about salvation beyond human history.

To summarize: I have suggested that a useful way conceptualize salvation is to think of it as the ultimate form of upward mobility and status transformation. Next, I framed the longstanding debates about the relative importance of *law and grace* in terms of how one obtains status by conformity and association. Most branches of the Christian church have emphasized the importance of an intimate relationship (i.e., association) with Jesus Christ as a gift of grace that transforms our spiritual status and makes salvation possible. If salvation is a free gift, however, does this make God's demand for justice irrelevant? If salvation is a gift available to both those who have followed God's commandments and those who have not, in what sense is God just? One way the church addressed this question is through the doctrine of *atonement*, which is usually linked to various forms of *sacrifice*. Finally, I discussed *eschatology*: how the church has envisioned life after death and the end of human history, and I argued that we need to be modest and reticent in what we assert about the realm beyond historical experience.

The purpose of using sociological concepts for theology is not to ban all traditional images, concepts, and interpretations. Rather, it is to suggest how we might think about these concepts without resorting to magic, but also to recognize the limits of human knowledge and the value of recognizing mystery. This is, of course, a theme of the entire book, but is especially relevant when we deal with the notion of salvation and related concepts.

The Problem of Evil and Tragedy

Why do innocent children suffer and die? Why are communities devastated by natural disasters and plagues? Why are the poor exploited by deceptive and usurious credit systems? Why have humans been involved in a near-endless number of wars? On a more

---

sociopolitical order (e.g., Isaiah 65:17; Romans 8:21; Revelations 21:1).

MORE DOCTRINES IN A NEW LANGUAGE

general level, the question is why there is so much evil and tragedy in the world? The line between evil and tragedy is not clearcut but as I use the terms here evil suggests that the bad outcome is the result of human intent. The Holocaust was evil. By tragedy I mean things that cause suffering but are not primarily due to human intent. Earthquakes are primarily tragic.

For Christians, this poses a related and even more difficult question. If God is omnipotent (all powerful) and omniscient (all knowing), how can she allow so much evil and tragedy in the world—and still be a loving God? This can lead to the conclusion that a loving, omnipotent, and omnificent God must not exist. Philosophers and logicians have elaborated various versions of this debate.[19] I will not try to even summarize these. Like the Clinton administration's policy about homosexuality in the military— "don't ask, don't tell"—Calvin's basic answer about why there is so much evil and tragedy was, "Don't ask, [God] won't tell."[20] That is, sinful humans should not question what the sovereign, all-powerful, and all-knowing God brings forth. God will not or cannot tell because God's ways are beyond human understanding.[21] Most moderns find this unsatisfying.

One source of evil is human sin, which was discussed above. If humans have freedom, this leaves open the possibility of not only sin, but of deliberate wickedness. If God did not give humans such freedom, they would be automatons, rather than creatures who can have a relationship with God. Their obedience and worship would be pointless. But such freedom can be misused by trying to become god-like. As noted in the section on sin, the tendency of

---

19. For a survey of such arguments see Tooley, *Problem of Evil*.

20. Wood, *Providence*, 91.

21. This theme of God's sovereignty and human's inability to fully understand God's ways runs through much of Calvin's *Institutes*. See, for example, book 1, chapter 16, section 9. It is perhaps most pronounced in his doctrine of election. While all are deserving of condemnation and perdition, some are from the beginning of creation elected (i.e., predestined) to salvation—and this has nothing to do with God's foreknowledge of how they will live their lives. (See, for example, book 3, chapter 22, section 1.) God's righteousness in such matters is not to be questioned.

humans to exalt themselves and to denigrate others is at the root of much of the evil in the world.

But human sin is not the only source of heartbreaking events. Why do diseases cause such suffering—even to innocent children? Why do natural disasters kill thousands of people who have done nothing special to deserve this—except be in the wrong place at the wrong time? Why do the good suffer and the evil prosper? Of course, humans may contribute to such outcomes by running risk for short-term material benefits. Nonetheless some tragic disasters are, according to both theology and the insurance industry, simply "acts of God." Why does an omnipotent, omniscient, and loving God allow such things?

Part of the problem hinges on what we mean by "omnipotent" and "omniscient." These concepts are not derived primarily from the Bible, but largely emerged from philosophical debates. As mentioned in the discussion of the Trinity, modern process theology has significantly qualified the extent to which God should be considered omnipotent and omniscient. Let me now suggest an imagery that may help to better understand the extent and the limits of God's power and the nature and source of evil.

Imagine God as the founder and chief executive officer (CEO) of a very large organization. (I know this sounds trite and banal but thinking of God as a king or a feudal "Lord" is no less banal!) Imagine someone who is head of an army, a corporation, a nation-state, or even a world government. Now imagine that she is the founder and CEO of the universe. This drastically, unimaginably increases the scope of her responsibilities. (There is no simple answer to how big our universe is, but it is billions and billions of light years wide.) While God the creator (i.e., founder) may have been instrumental in creating and shaping the universe, he is limited by his own creation. Having brought about the "big bang" or evolution, he cannot stop the playing out of the consequences. Bill Gates cannot suddenly transform Microsoft into Exxon or the Catholic Church. Like all heads of complex organizations, God may have to make some tough, even tragic decisions, just as an army general may have to decide to sacrifice the lives of the people in a squad in order to save a regiment and win a battle. A ruling politician may have to decide to spend money on limiting terrorism rather than on children's health care. Even if the general and politician were to reverse their decisions, the outcomes are likely to be tragic for some. Of course, to the degree that God is the creator of the universe or the ground of being, the "decisions" and "trade-offs" that have to be made are infinitely more complex and even incomprehensible. All of this is to say that instead of omnipotent, we should think of God as supremely powerful, but limited because of past decisions and commitments—such as establishing natural laws and giving humans a certain kind of freedom. As already discussed when we considered the doctrine of providence, God is further limited because she has chosen to influence and be influenced primarily by symbolic communications such as prayer, meditation, bodily movements, and the sacraments. Similarly, God may know all her creatures, but that does not mean she can completely anticipate the future—for God, as well as the rest of existence, is in process. Supreme knowledge is not total knowledge about the future.

The God of the eighteenth-century deists was like a clock maker who constructs a machine and then leaves it to run on its own; their God was largely detached from subsequent events. In contrast, the CEO image leaves God the power to intervene through symbolic interactions with devotees and sees God as one who cares about what happens to humans.

Now let me say quickly that God as a founder and CEO is only a metaphor, and like all metaphors it is limited in its accuracy and usefulness. It does, however, recognize both God's supremacy and her substantial but limited ability to protect humans from all forms of evil.

Even "hard-nosed" CEOs may have genuine sympathy for those who are negatively affected by their decisions. Even if they are insensitive to their employee's needs, CEOs usually have families and friends they care about. They may very well offer genuine concern and support when others suffer: the wife who develops cancer, the teenage daughter who is raped, and the parent who has Alzheimer's.

If in some ways God is like a CEO, she is also like a spouse: the wife who comforts our failures, the husband who nurses us back to health, or the companion who knows some of our deepest secrets. If supremacy is one characteristic, intimacy is another.

In the Catholic tradition, the Virgin Mary serves as the sympathetic quasi-deity who intervenes for vulnerable human beings when they approach the almighty God as creator and ruler. In a sense she has served not only as "Holy Mary, mother of God," but as the unofficial loving and sympathetic divine mother to human beings. For a number of reasons, the Virgin Mary is a problematic image and metaphor for most Protestants. This is why I have suggested the loving spouse as the symbol of intimacy rather than the mother or parent, but parental images may be more powerful for some people.

One thing that Jesus's crucifixion symbolizes is God participating in human suffering. Much of contemporary theology calls into question the idea that God is impassible (i.e., immune from pain or injury). Rather, God is with us sharing our suffering and offering comfort and support. This is a crucial role of the doctrine of incarnation. God is not only with us, but also like us: vulnerable. This is a powerful metaphor that suggests God's love and concern for us.

Many scholars referred to the attempt to answer the question of why God permits evil as *theodicy*. Strictly speaking, I have not tried to solve the contradiction theodicy points to: an all-powerful, loving God and the existence of so much evil. Rather, like other contemporary theologians, I have qualified God's omnipotence and omniscience. Of course, the imagery of a CEO of the universe and a loving spouse do not fully solve the problem. For while Calvin's "don't ask, won't tell" is inadequate, there is a sense in which we cannot and should not attempt to eliminate the mystery that is at the center of Divine-human relationships. Such a strategy recognizes both the usefulness of human language, rationality, and anthropomorphic images of God—and their limits.

Now we turn from doctrines, metaphors and symbolism to the central activity of the church: worship.

Chapter 7

Worship[1]

In theistic religions God is the One Who is Worshipped. This is some sort of a definition. We have, therefore, only to find out what worship is to know the proper use of the name "God."

—CHARLES HARTSHORNE[2]

THE MOST COMMON WAY for people to experience the redemptive power of theism is through periodic worship services—Sunday services for Christians, pujas for Hindus, Friday Salat for Muslims, Sabbath services for Jews, and the like.[3] Worship is not primar-

---

1. This discussion of worship and the following discussion of salvation draw heavily on my article "Status and Sacredness: Worship and Salvation" and my book *Status and Sacredness*, ch. 13.

2. Hartshorne, *Natural Theology for Our Time*, 3. I do not mean to imply that the role Hartshorne attributes to worship is the same as my analysis suggests. He was much more wed to the religious significance of metaphysics and logic than I am. For example, he says, "Eventually we may all, in East and West, hope to reach better understanding concerning the role of logic in religious thought. Intuition is valuable, and indeed indispensable; but I have a certain faith in the rights and duties of rational metaphysical inquiry..." (p. 24). I have less faith in this kind of argumentation on sociological grounds: it has done little to revitalize theology for people in the pew. While process theology has been influential among some Christian intellectuals, I see little indication that it has slowed the decline of religious commitment in Western societies or significantly improved the understanding of those who still attend Christian worship.

3. While the Hindu puja should be done daily, and Sunni Muslim should do the salat five times a day, it is still the case that for Hindus going to a temple

83

ily a matter of learning meditation techniques from a guru or of an individual praying; rather they are social and collective events. Participation in such services usually is the key distinguishing characteristic of the religious person. A high proportion of the resources of religious institutions go into carrying out these periodic services. A sociology of worship can help us to better understand both the similarities and the differences in worship practices across religious traditions—and contribute to a clearer and more systematic theology of worship.

"Worship" as used here is not synonymous with religious ritual. Some rituals are primarily magic: attempts to manipulate gods, spirits, and devils. They can amount to a form of coercion—forcing the gods to do something by conducting the right rituals or knowing a secret mantra. Other rituals amount to tit-for-tat bargaining—if God will do this for me, I will do this in return. Worship in its pure form is adoration of God without the expectation of any concrete return—just as the Christian concept of grace refers to God's unmerited gifts to humans. A worldly analogy of worship is expressing admiration of a famous person without expecting that person to reply. Both God and the famous person are worthy of praise because of who they are and what they have *already* done.

In its most general sense, people worship what they consider sacred, that to which they attribute the highest status. This can be their family, career, country, or property, rather than what is normally thought of as a god. In the narrower and more traditional sense, worship usually refers to ritualized acts of deference and intimacy with something that is considered to transcend the profane world. This ritualized action is intended to both maintain and affirm the status of what is considered sacred, and to transform the status of the devotee. Typically worship involves three key processes.

---

and for Muslims attending Friday prayers in a mosque are of special significance. In part this is because these are publicly visible acts of devotion and the simultaneous acts of other worshipers contribute to emotional impact and social legitimacy of this kind of religious activity. Of course, Sabbath services have long been the central part of Jewish and Christian devotion.

WORSHIP

Preparation and Confession

In sociological terms, preparation for worship usually involves distancing oneself from past acts of deviance and reaffirming the (religious) groups' norms. Preparation may involve ascetic practices such as fasting or silence, which distance one from typical daily concerns. Physical purity is a frequent symbol.[4] For example, taking off one's shoes symbolizes reducing one's association with the most common point of contact with the profane and dirty world. "Then [God] said, [to Moses] 'come no closer! Remove your sandals, for the place on which you are standing is holy ground'" (Exodus 3:5; see also Joshua 5:15 and Acts 7:33). Another even more common symbol is washing or bathing. This may be literal, as when the Hindu bathes and puts on clean clothes before a puja. It can be both literal and symbolic, as when Sunni Muslims wash parts of their body before praying. Or it may be strictly symbolic, as when traditional Catholics dip their fingers in holy water and make the sign of the cross as they enter the church. The most important symbol of cleansing for Christians is baptism, a ritual of purification that is usually a requirement to fully participate in the life of a church.

Another form of getting ready is preparing a proper place of worship. You're not likely to meet the pope or the president of a major country at the local McDonald's. Exalted people usually meet in a high status or special place. So do gods and devotees: "And [God said] have them make me a sanctuary, so that I may dwell among them" (Exodus 25:8). Hindu temples, Muslim mosques, Sikh gurdwaras, Buddhist stupas, Jewish synagogues, and Christian churches are all special places for meditation and worship. After you have gotten to know God at the local place of worship, you may also be aware of her presence at the McDonald's, but the reverse is not usually the case.

When going to meet a very high-status person or entering a high-status place, lower-status individuals usually "dress up";

---

4. See Douglas, *Purity and Danger*, for a classic discussion of the symbolism of purity.

the term itself is instructive. When people interact with those of especially high status, they tend to use formal or special language (e.g., "Mr. President," "Your Honor," "Your Holiness"). They are more likely to mention their high-status mentors and friends, not their favorite prostitute or drug dealer. Similarly, worshipers usually attempt to shed the worst aspects of their personhood or soul. That is, they attempt to better conform to the norms of their religious community in order to be worthy of coming into the presence of their god.

For Christians, the above processes are symbols for distancing the devotee from their sins and preparing them to come into the presence of the Holy. This is why some form of confession usually comes relatively early in a Christian worship service. For example, "Almighty God, unto whom all hearts are open, all desires known, and from whom no secrets are hid: Cleanse the thoughts of our hearts by the inspiration of thy Holy Spirit, that we may perfectly love thee and worthily magnify thy holy name." Versions of this are used by a number of Christian denominations. The congregation acknowledges individual and collective sins and asks forgiveness and absolution. This may include prayers, hymns, and bodily movements (e.g., bowing, kneeling, beating the breast or lying prostrate). Some Christian traditions (e.g., Baptists and Pentecostals) may use less formal and more spontaneous ways of expressing preparation and confession, but nearly all kinds of Christian worship seek to acknowledge sin, reaffirm the groups' norms, renew their efforts to conform to these norms, and thereby repair the worshipers' spiritual status.

Praise of the Deity

Sociologically speaking, the higher the status of the superior, the more the lower-status actor is transformed by an association. A servant of the king has a higher status than the servant of a small farmer. Therefore, the lower-status actor has an interest in their superior maintaining and increasing her status. But this is too simple and too cynical an account of why inferiors praise superiors;

inferiors may truly admire superiors and be grateful for the help and support they have been given. Good and generous mentors are often truly appreciated by those they have helped long after the mentor is useful to them.

To put this in religious language, such relationships frequently involve acts of grace that are unmerited gifts. And the disciples respond with genuine praise and gratitude. Hence, the second common element of worship is praise and adoration of the deity. Many of the psalms express this:

> It is good to give thanks to the Lord
>> to sing praises to your name, O Most High
> to declare your steadfast love in the morning,
>> and your faithfulness by night,
> to the music of the lute and the harp,
>> to the melody of the lyre,
> For you, O Lord, have made me glad by your work:
>> at the work of your hands I sing for joy.
> How great are your works, O Lord!
>> Your thoughts are very deep!
>
> (Psalm 92:1–5)

Many Protestant hymns also express similar notions of adoration. One of the most popular hymns begins, "Holy, holy, holy! Lord God, Almighty!" Later the hymn expresses the distance between God and all else: "only thou art holy, there is none beside thee perfect in power, in love and purity."[5] So, one crucial aspect of worship is to recognize the otherness of what is worshipped. If it is not "other" the worship may be engaging in idolatry.

---

5. The hymn was written by Reginald Heber, bishop of Calcutta (now Kolkata) (1783–1826). It quotes the Sanctus of the Latin Mass and also paraphrases Revelation 4:1–11.

Intimacy with the Deity

Worship services often culminate with a renewed sense of intimacy with one's god. As the earlier discussion of how status systems work indicated, eating and sex are often key symbols of intimate associations. For certain branches of Hinduism, especially sects that focus on Krishna, both women and men devotees are to imagine that they are lovers to their god, and the sexual imagery is quite explicit. In certain orders of Catholic nuns, a symbol of devotion is becoming married to Jesus—often symbolized by a wedding ring. Common to both Catholic and Protestants is conceptualizing the church as the "bride of Christ." Thus, sexual imagery symbolizing intimacy with God is found in a variety of religious traditions.

Much more common is the notion of a meal with one's god as a sign of intimacy. This is found in most Christian churches in the Eucharist, also called the Lord's Supper or Communion. This practice is the climax of most worship services in the Catholic and Anglican traditions. In other traditions the Eucharist is conducted less frequently, but even in the Baptist tradition it is seen as a means of intimacy. In the *Baptist Hymnal* the first hymn in the section on the "Lord's Supper" begins, "Where can we find thee, Lord, so near, So real, so gracious, so divine, As at the table set with love, By those who know themselves as thine?"[6]

In church traditions that place less emphasis on the Lord's Supper, there are other important ways to express intimacy with God. Prayers tend to be less formal and take the form of a conversation with God: "Lord, we just want to ask you to be with us . . ." and "Thank you Jesus for all you have done for us . . ." Often such intimacy is expressed in songs: ". . . He walked with me and he talked with me, and he told me I was his own . . ."[7] Among Pentecostal churches, becoming possessed by the Holy Spirit and "speaking in tongues" is a key form of intimacy with God.

---

6. *Baptist Hymnal*, 245.

7. These are words from the gospel song "I Come to the Garden Alone," written by American songwriter C. Austin Miles (1868–1946), which was and is very popular in some Christian traditions.

Though there are alternative ways to experience and symbolize intimacy with God, in nearly all traditions this is a key goal of worship. The result is that this intimacy renews and strengthens one's association with God. It is this intimate association that transforms the status and personhood of the devotee.

Brief Notes on Sacrifice, Prayer, Preaching, and Mysticism

As noted above, sacrifice can be a matter of magical coercion or quid pro quo exchange, as well as worship per se. In worship, sacrifice and prayer can express any one or all three of the elements previously identified: purification, praise, and intimacy. As discussed in the section on atonement, *sacrifice* is probably so common in religious traditions because it symbolizes a number of different processes: casting away sin, offering a gift, intimacy with the deity, etc. As noted earlier, the same is true of *prayer*; there are prayers of preparation, prayers of praise and adoration, prayers of petition, and prayers expressing intimacy. Similarly, preaching and deferential listening to preaching can express all three of these elements.

Mysticism tends to emphasize the limits of language and the human mind in grasping the nature of worship and of God. The *Oxford English Dictionary* defines mysticism as: "belief in the possibility of union with or absorption into God by means of contemplation and self-surrender; belief in or devotion to the spiritual apprehension of truths inaccessible to the intellect."[8] There are many, many forms of mysticism both within Christianity and in many other religious traditions.[9] What they seem to have in common is a sense that language and logical discussion

---

8. The first *OED* definition is frequently derogatory: "Religious belief that is characterized by vague, obscure, or confused spirituality; a belief system based on the assumption of occult forces, mysterious supernatural agencies, etc."

9. For a useful overview of mysticism see Smart, *Mysticism*. For a sense of the scope and variety of mysticism see the series of books edited by Steven T. Katz and published by Oxford University Press.

are not a sufficient means for developing a deep relationship with God. Instead, the emphasis seems to be on disciplined practices of prayer, meditation, and daily life leading to an abandonment of the soul to God. The goal is intimacy with God that goes beyond any analogy with human relationships. The devotee develops a sense or consciousness of the presence of God. Some traditions see this as leading to uniting with or being absorbed by God—though most forms of mysticism would reject such notions. On the one hand, mysticism stresses the importance of intimate associations with the deity. Many forms of mysticism stress the importance of disciplined conformity to certain rules and techniques to accomplish this intimate association. The content of these rules and techniques can vary enormously depending on the particular religious tradition. The result of such techniques can involve not only a consciousness of the presence of God, but extraordinary events such as hearing God's voice and seeing visions. Mysticism is often associated with monasticism or special communities. This is because the discipline and techniques usually require the devotee to be free from distraction and to spend considerable time learning the practices needed to sense God's presence. While a long tradition within Christianity, mysticism has usually been practiced by a relatively small minority of those who would call themselves Christians. While small groups of laity may engage in mystical practices, mysticism is not central to most forms of congregational worship in the modern period.

This book takes the alternative approach to most forms of mysticism. While recognizing the limits of language and clarity, I attempt to use a new language to make many of the traditional doctrines more intelligible to contemporary people. I do not reject the legitimacy or usefulness of mysticism, but I do want to point to its tendency toward monasticism and religious elitism, and the problems this creates for most people in contemporary society.

Varieties of Worship Styles

It is obvious that there are significant differences between a Catholic high mass, Bible study in a house church, and speaking in tongues in a Pentecostal service. True worship can take place in any of these—and many other settings. Which style of worship people find most satisfying is shaped by their social background, their current social context, and variations in personality. Each style has virtues as well as dangers. Hence, we should expect a variety of forms and styles.[10]

This is not to say that anything goes. In judging the legitimacy of different styles, we should be suspicious if they tend toward magic, bargaining, idolatry or involve violence. An important contemporary movement that comes perilously close to the tit-for-tat model is the Prosperity Gospel, whose "good news" is that spiritual faithfulness will lead to economic prosperity. Another common danger is for worship to become a performance or entertainment event, like going to the movies or a concert. This is especially a temptation in contemporary megachurches, though not all megachurches are necessarily guilty of this.

A second form of idolatry is to confuse familiarity and comfortableness with sacredness; this is probably the special temptation of mainline churches, especially those that have highly standardized

---

10. After this book was in press, I read Theo Hobson's *Reinventing Liberal Christianity* (2013). To greatly simplify his arguments, he defends the liberal democratic state (though not neoliberal capitalism) as the polity most favorable for contemporary Christianity. This is in contrast to pacifists like Stanley Hauerwas (*Resident Aliens*) and advocates of radical orthodoxy like John Milbank (*Theology and Social Theory*), Graham Ward (*Postmodern God*), and (probably) Rowan Williams (*Tokens of Trust*). I largely agree with Hobson on this point, though the church will at times have to adapt to, though not approve of, more authoritarian regimes. His second key point—and the reason I mention him in this chapter—is that the church must move toward a more "cultic" form of worship that centers on the Eucharist and often may resemble emotion-laden public spectacles more than traditional church worship services. He appears to be advocating a "one size fits all" approach to worship. For the reasons discussed in this chapter, people with different experiences and different social backgrounds are likely to be attracted to different styles of worship so I am skeptical of Hobson's attempt to reinvent worship.

services. A third kind of idolatry is to worship the Bible (or selected translations or portions of the Bible, or a particular prayer book, or a particular creed) rather than God. A former pastor of mine tells the story of a Christmas Eve service in which he read the traditional story of Jesus's birth (Luke 2:1–20). An obviously unhappy visitor exited shaking his head and all he said was, "Swaddling clothes, swaddling clothes," perturbed that the New Revised Standard Version translates this as "bands of cloth."

The point of worship is renewal and transformation, a renewed awareness of God's status, availability, and grace, and of both our failings and our possibilities. Intimate association with our God transforms our spiritual status, who we are, and how we relate to others.

But no matter what style is used and how faithfully worship is performed, profane day-to-day life reasserts itself, the human experience of contingency and powerlessness continues, and awareness of God's availability is eroded. The transformation of the person and the world that results from worship is only temporary. This is one of the reasons worship and other rituals need to be repeated again and again—and why they are so central to the life of the church.

Expressing and Confessing Our Faith

If the theology—the more formal and lengthy expositions of faith—needs new languages, so do our prayers and our statements of faith that are recited in worship. Very few lay men and women are likely to spend much time reading theology books. Many do think about the creeds and prayers that they recite. What follows is one attempt to restate the Lord's Prayer and a Confession of Faith that tries to take into account both the church's tradition *and* the need for more contemporary worship aids.

WORSHIP

The Lord's Prayer

O God, our Father and Mother who transcends this world,

Holy and sacred is your name.

May the commonwealth you envision come to pass.

And may your will be done,

both in the world we know and in worlds beyond.

Provide us our needs for this day.

Forgive us our failings,

as we forgive those who failed us.

Lead us away from temptation and evil,

For only with your love and power can we be redeemed.

A Confession of Faith

Minister: *Let us confess our faith.*

All:
We believe in God who nurtures and guides us,
We know God through
> Jesus and the Holy Spirit,
> the Holy Scriptures,
> the kindness of others,
> the gift of our children,
> the wonders of nature,
> and in many other ways.

We were given great potential,
> but we deeply compromise this by our pride and insecurity.

We often fail to do what our better selves intend,

and we are saddened by our weakness, failure, and malice

We affirm that Jesus Christ is crucial to our understanding of God.

He combined the characteristics of both humanity and divinity.

His concern for the sick, the poor, and the disreputable,

and his demand for justice

led to his death on a cross.

Following his death, the disciples had extraordinary experiences, which they described as the Resurrection.

These experiences continue to shape the church and our lives.

We experience God's presence

in the life of the church and in collective worship,

where we sense intimacy with God through

prayer, Scripture, preaching, music, and the Eucharist.

We recommit ourselves

to follow in the way of Jesus

to renew our openness to God's healing love

to improve our troubled and complex world,

to cooperate with all seeking to create a more loving community, and

to recognize that we can only accomplish these things by the grace of God.

Minister: *"Go on your way; your faith has made you well."* (Luke 17:19)

Now we turn to the most fundamental question that confronts any theistic theology: is there a God?

Chapter 8

Is There a God?

Commitment Despite Doubt

THE PREVIOUS PARTS OF the book suggest how sociological concepts might be applied to theological issues. Most of the above discussion assumes (1) that there is a God, (2) that humans can have a supremely significant relationship with God, and (3) that in some (but not all) respects this relationship is analogous to interaction between human actors. This also assumes that this God that is not simply a figment of some humans' imagination. This raises what for many is the fundamental question: can reasonable contemporary human beings affirm the reality of God?

One response is to draw on William Irwin's formulation: to think of "God as a question, not an answer." Irwin proclaims himself to be an atheist, but he argues that both believers and atheists are subject to doubt. He asserts, "Belief without doubt would not be required by an all-loving God." Cast iron certainty "should not be worn as a badge of honor. Any honest atheist must admit that he has his doubts. . . . Anyone who does not occasionally worry that she is wrong about the existence or nonexistence of God most likely has a fraudulent belief." I will refer to the perspective Irwin outlines as *"commitment despite doubt."* Irwin then goes on to cite the Trappist monk Thomas Merton, who argued that "faith is a decision, a judgment that is fully and deliberately taken in light of a truth that cannot be proven . . ."[1]

---

1. Irwin, *God Is a Question*. As Irwin indicates the title is a line from one of the characters in Albert Camus' *The Stranger*.

There is no way to be certain that this perspective of "commitment despite doubt" is correct, but this accords with my own experience. More important, this stance reflects an appropriate level of intellectual humility. The acknowledgement of some inevitable doubt does not mean people do not vary in how confident they are about the faith decision they have made or that most people are in constant turmoil about their faith.

An example of the most skeptical version of "commitment despite doubt" is found in Colson Whitehead's novel *The Underground Railroad*, when a character says: "Sometimes a useful delusion is better than a useless truth."[2] My point is that, for some questions, no clear line exists between certainty, doubt, and useful illusion—or even a delusion. Humans make an existential decision about what they think about God and how this will shape their lives, and perhaps their afterlives.

If the first step is to treat the existence of God as a question that cannot be answered in any definitive way by rational argument, the next step is to decide how to respond to this situation and this question. In the section that follows I will argue that most (and probably all) encompassing views of human existence involve important faith commitments.

Faith Responses

Without claiming that this exhausts the possibilities, I will sketch out three classic faith responses. I refer to these as Stoicism, Epicureanism, and Theism. (One indication that these three traditions are "classic" is found in Acts 17: 18, which reports that Paul debated with Stoic and Epicurean philosophers when he was in Athens. So, the comparison I am making is not a new one). Each of the three traditions has many variations and subtypes. My use of these labels is broader than the historical traditions that scholars usually associate with the terms. While I will identify what I see as core ideas in each of these, this does not mean that

---

2. Whitehead, *Underground Railroad*.

these ideas or themes are totally absent from the other types of commitments. Some of these terms are conventionally capitalized and some are not; for consistency, I will capitalize all three terms. My claim is that all three of these traditions involve faith assumptions that cannot be proven or disproven—and these assumptions shape the way we live.

The first type I refer to as *Stoicism*. Many varieties of Western Stoicism have a relatively pantheistic concept of God—God is another name for the universe or nature—and the goal is to be in congruence with the nature-given realities of the particular situations that confront one. There is a strong elitist strain in this perspective in that only sages are likely to control their desires and passions sufficiently to reach the desired outcome of being immune to misfortune. Others are unhappy; they are controlled by their desires and passions, which eventually lead to disappointment and frustration. Many varieties of Hinduism and Buddhism have strong parallels with Western Stoicism.[3] First, they share a rather tragic and resigned view of earthly existence—suffering is at the core of human experience.[4] Sometimes this is defined as "realism." The emphasis on "realism" can lapse into forms of fatalism.[5] Second, individuals are responsible for training themselves to be without passion, for this is the best defense against suffering. For classic Stoicism,

---

3. Some *bhakit* sects in Hinduism are an exception, though the ones that solely emphasize grace have a rather limited following. See my discussion of this in my *Status and Sacredness*, 197–202. The same is true for certain Buddhist traditions, but even where grace rather than works is emphasized, the world is still basically evil; it is thought of as a "burning house" from which the Buddha will rescue the believer.

4. The accomplished sage may not perceive their situation as tragic, but a perspective that sees most people as mired in suffering can hardly be called optimistic.

5. In the Hindu tradition, this is expressed in the notion of different ages (*yugas*), with each stage more corrupted than the previous one. It is also expressed in the injunction to carry out the duties (dharma) associated with one's social roles—especially duties associated with one's caste—without worrying about the consequences for yourself or others. For an elaboration and clarification of Hindu perspectives on this, see my *Status and Sacredness*, 45 and 78 (on *yugas*) and 190–203 (on *dharma*).

this is accomplished through disciplined reason that protects the sage from misfortune and provides some peace of mind. For many forms of Hinduism and Buddhism, this is accomplished primarily through various kinds of meditation. These often involve training both the mind and the body. The many varieties of yoga are the most famous of these techniques. The emphasis is on controlling the passions, by controlling not only the body but also the mind. For many forms of these religions the idea of detachment or nonattachment from the world and human relationships is the ideal.[6] This sometimes includes detaching from concept of the self. This attempt to control the passions has sometimes led to extreme, even bizarre, forms of asceticism. Other traditions, such as Pure Land tradition of Mahayana Buddhism, allow for the role of a mediator and hence a kind of spiritual relationship. In short, whether or not there is a God, or gods, or a mediator, humans will experience misfortune and suffering and individuals are responsible for developing techniques to minimize this. In some parts of the Buddhist tradition, only a small elite—analogous to the Stoic sages—will be capable of attaining the desired state.

A second type of faith response is *Epicureanism*. Gods may exist, but they are largely indifferent to human lives. Hence, the appropriate goal for humans is to seek happiness. Happiness has multiple sources including satisfying the physical senses, which is considered appropriate and good. According to most forms of Epicureanism, seeking physical pleasure should be done in moderation; overindulgence leads to unhappiness. For Epicurus, the founder of this school, friendship is perhaps the most satisfying activity. When happiness becomes focused on maximizing physical pleasure and minimizing pain, it becomes hedonism. This perspective also comes in a variety of forms and rationales. Hedonism often assumes that the human condition is finite and without transcendent meaning, justifying some version of "eat, drink, and be merry, for tomorrow we die," a notion that is reported in the Bible (Ecclesiastes 8:15; Isaiah 22:13; Luke 12:19). This worldview has

---

6. For a discussion of this issue in Buddhism see Burley, *Petrification*, 204–8; and Huntington, "Triumph of Narcissism," 624–48.

IS THERE A GOD?

an inherent tendency to desensitize its followers to the needs of others and issues of social justice.

Obviously, my description of Stoicism and Epicureanism oversimplifies the complexities of the various traditions that I characterize with these terms; nonetheless, this is a legitimate characterization of the central tendencies of particular stances toward the human experience. Such stances are existential faith commitments.

I would argue that most modern secular thought—some of which is anti-religious and some simply agnostic or indifferent—is typically a combination of Stoicism and Epicureanism. The Stoic element of modern thought asserts that there is no meaning to the universe and human existence—except that created by humans. We need to "stoically" face up to this and "learn to live with it." The Epicurean element of contemporary culture says, "So what if existence has no meaning or direction, and the sun will burnout in five billion years. Relax, enjoy yourself!" Humans should concentrate on making themselves as happy as we can. This can include a concern for social justice as a strategy for maximizing collective happiness and can involve moderation in the pursuit of pleasure.

Just as Theism can be used to justify religious fanaticism, Stoicism can lead to resignation, hopelessness and despair. Epicureanism can lead to hedonism, which easily becomes a rationale for self-indulgence and the treatment of others as objects. The most pervasive and influential ideology of the contemporary world is *consumer capitalism*,[7] which is now a largely secular perspective that draws on the assumptions of both these traditions. Like the sages of Stoicism and Buddhism, modern humans should learn to deal with the often-harsh realities of life. The techniques for doing this may be different—drugs, psychotherapy, changing jobs or spouses—but we are each responsible for creating our own

---

7. As Max Weber pointed out, there are various forms of capitalism that tend to be associated with particular time periods and geographical areas. Some of these include booty capitalism (often linked to piracy), merchant capitalism, industrial capitalism, consumer capitalism, and financial capitalism. Each of these terms indicate the core activity in acquiring profit that is characteristic of a locale or period.

meaningful life. One way of coping with meaninglessness is to follow the Epicurean emphasis on seeking our happiness through pursuing pleasure. In the modern context this means pursuing an ever-increasing level of consumption. This usually is closely linked to seeking a more elevated social status. In the context of consumer capitalism, the display of commodities plays a central role in gaining status.

The concern with consumption and status is accentuated by a major industry and academic discipline called "marketing," which is largely devoted to convincing people they need more "stuff." For example, a key slogan of Mail Chimp, a leading email marketing company, is: "Send better emails; sell more stuff." Marketing is assisted by another industry called "advertising," which often draws on those with artistic talent and plays a major role in shaping popular culture. On a collective level, these Epicurean impulses take the form of a preoccupation with economic growth—the idol of most contemporary societies. For example, in the ideologically polarized U.S. of the 2016 election, there was little agreement about anything, except that more economic growth was desirable; the debate was over how to accomplish this.

A third faith response is some form of *Theism* in which a God has an ongoing relationship with humans. This is characteristic of all branches of the Abrahamic faiths, Judaism, Christianity, and Islam, as well as a variety of other religious traditions. The nature of the divine-human relationship and the degree to which the deity intervenes in physical processes and human history can vary significantly for these different traditions. Some of these issues were discussed in the sections on providence and revelation. As noted in chapter 3, theism can be a potential poison or tranquillizer leading to fanaticism or conventionality. Another temptation is naïve optimism. This can take diverse forms. Some Christians quote Paul's phrase "We know that all things work together for good to those who love God" without remembering that this comes in the context of Paul's deep awareness of sin, of the crucifixion, and of the persecution of the first century churches. Two modern versions of naïve optimism are Norman Vincent Peale's *The Power of*

IS THERE A GOD?

Positive Thinking and, as mentioned above, the "Prosperity Gospel." There is an element of truth in the idea that certain forms of naiveté and optimism can have positive effects. First, optimism can be a useful counterpoint to the kind of realism that lapses into Machiavellian cynicism. If we reject any notion of a better future, it will not occur. Second, optimism gives a greater capacity to deal with terrible circumstances.

But Christian Theism does not offer optimism, per se; it offers hope—a hope that does not ignore tragedy but helps us to deal with it. Nelson Mandela and Bishop Tutu had the seemingly naïve hope that South African apartheid could be ended without widespread bloodshed—and their hope played a vital role in bringing this about. Empirical research also indicates that those with hope and a positive attitude are more likely to survive serious illnesses, to overcome academic handicaps, to deal with economic distress, and, in general, to increase the chances of positive outcomes.[8]

The key point is that all three of the traditions sketched above involve faith assumptions—that is, the way people respond to the mysteriousness of existence and to the uncertainties and tragedies of human life. None of these perspectives is necessarily either pro- or anti-science, though particular forms of any of these three can be pre- or even anti-scientific.

Atheists and skeptics have long been present in most societies, but in the twenty-first century a new, more aggressive form of atheism has emerged. This is referred to in the mass media as "the New Atheism." New Atheists tend to have a high

---

8. There are many research articles on these issues, and while admittedly the quality of the research is highly variable, the positive effect of hope and optimism are a consistent finding. Some examples of this research include:

Patelli and Pedrini, "Is the Optimism Sincere?"
McCoy and Bowen, "Hope in the Social Environment."
Phan, "Longitudinal Examination of Optimism."
Buyukgoze-Kavas, "Predicting Career Adaptability."
Hong et al., "Spirituality, Hope, and Self-Sufficiency."
Kılınç, "Teacher Academic Optimism and School Climate."
Kivima, "Optimism and Pessimism as Predictors."
Mondloch et al., "Does How You Do Depend. . . ?"

degree of confidence in the intellectual positions they advocate. They criticize religion in ways that border on intolerance. Probably the most famous of these advocates are Richard Dawkins, Christopher Hitchens, Sam Harris, and Daniel Dennett.[9] What is troubling, from my point of view, is the near-absolutism and the debasing of all other forms of knowledge. This is itself a particular kind of unacknowledged faith assumption, sometimes bordering on fanaticism. Just as the most radical and intolerant voices of religionists do not represent most people of faith, the New Atheists do not represent the average atheist. The problem with either overly passionate religious or anti-religious advocates is that they, usually inadvertently, provide legitimacy to those who would persecute those who do not agree with them.

Why this detour through three classic perspectives? The key point is that all of these involve faith assumptions.

Is God a Creation of Humans?

The classic critics of religion, including Feuerbach, Marx, and Freud, have suggested that gods are human projections: people attribute life and activity to imaginary beings. It can be likened to a child who thinks of their doll as a real actor that provides them companionship and comfort. The critics of religion vary in why and how these projections come about, but they all assume that the imagined beings are unreal human creations.

Emile Durkheim argues that such dismissals of religion are misguided. The sacred beings and objects are crucial symbols for something that is real: the human group or society that shares these symbols. (His analysis focuses on religion in the small aboriginal groups of Australia in which the sacred object is usually a totem, such as an animal. He considers these tribal practices to represent *The Elementary Forms of Religious Life*—the title of his book on this subject). According to Durkheim, such symbols are a crucial basis of social solidarity. This solidarity occurs primarily

---

9. For an overview of this movement, see Taylor, "The New Atheists."

IS THERE A GOD?

by two mechanisms. First, individual and social differences within the groups are minimized by the total otherness of the sacred god or object. (This is analogous to the way that differences within a group may be minimized in the face of a common enemy or the way fans—with little else in common— find solidarity in their appreciation of a particular celebrity.) Second, solidarity is built by collective rituals. Sacred gods and objects produce awe and wonder and should be treated with respect and deference. This usually takes the form of some type of religious ritual. Over time, norms emerge about what constitutes appropriate forms of deference. These become codified into rituals that usually involve both language and body movements. Some rituals are carried out in private, but the most powerful rituals are performed by a group. Durkheim refers to such a group as a "church." The shared awe toward a sacred symbol and the periodic repetition of these rituals produce a shared emotional experience that contributes to social solidarity. This is seen not only in what is traditionally defined as religious worship, but also in coordinated cheering at sporting events, saying the "Pledge of Allegiance" at school, singing the national anthem at ballgames, and watching military parades. Social scientists generally agree that notions of the sacred and the mechanisms that Durkheim identified do contribute to social solidarity. What is more dubious is Durkheim's disingenuous argument that religion is not based on an illusion. Rather, what he is really arguing is that while people think they are worshipping a god or sacred totem, what they are "really" worshiping is the social group to which they belong.

My own position is that, in the context of science, much religious behavior can be "explained" in relatively "naturalistic" terms. A "real" God is not needed as an explanation of much of religious behavior. Repeating what I said in chapter 2, there is some debate about exactly what "explain" means.[10] A common implication is that an explanation provides a linked description. Such a description

---

10. This understanding of explanation is not without its critics, which include both various forms of *historicism* and *historism*. A discussion of these perspectives is not required for my present purposes.

enables the analysts to make predictions about events that have not yet occurred—or more accurately, have not been previously observed—and hence cannot have affected the formulation of the theory that is being testing. Magic draws on pseudo-explanations and historic religions have often used significant amounts of magic (e.g., attempts to use rituals to bring rain). But a theology that will appeal to and sustain modern educated people must avoid magic. Science, and the knowledge it produces, is not the only context in which humans live and operate. Theology deals with questions that are to a significant degree beyond the scope of science. For me this includes: why does anything exist; how should we relate our small planet and its life-forms to the incredibly vast universe; does existence including human history have any meaning; and how do we best cope with the contingencies and tragedies of life: illness and pain, our anticipated death and the death of those we love, ruptured relationships, and natural disasters? In my opinion, better scientific theories and more data can, at best, only partially answer most of these questions. Rather, what is required is an existential answer to what one perceives as the best way to live in a vast, complex, and still mysterious universe. When I refer to "an existential answer," I do not mean that a person's response is unrelated to their social and historical background. Human decisions are always some combination of our genetic inheritance, the culture from which we come, the structures that make up our immediate context, our past life experiences, and human freedom and choice. I have sketched out three classic responses: Stoicism, Epicureanism, and Theism. I opt for a form of Theism. More specifically, I have both grown up in and chosen a particular variety of Christian Theism: liberal Protestantism. Other thoughtful and well-intended people will make other choices. Their right to make such choices should be respected. This does not necessarily mean we respect their "gods" or the behavior that results from their choice—especially if they lead to violence and injustice toward others. Still, we must acknowledge that non-Christian and non-religious choices can be legitimate. But following Joshua (24:15) we can proclaim, ". . . choose for yourselves this day whom you will serve . . . But as for me and my household, we will serve the Lord."

Perhaps a more modern version of this might be: We respect the right of others to choose their ultimate concern. But, as Christians, we choose to draw on the healing and redeeming higher power that we have experienced in the life and death of Jesus Christ, and his resurrection in the church, the living Body of Christ.

Chapter 9

Conclusion

A KEY PURPOSE OF this book has been to suggest concepts, metaphors, and images that make liberal versions of Christianity more understandable and more persuasive. I have drawn on concepts from sociology to restate many of the traditional Christian doctrines. I make no claim this is the only appropriate language for theology. Rather, I see this approach as one useful set of concepts that can be used—often metaphorically—to explain much of Christian doctrine. Perhaps some classical doctrines need to be completely abandoned, but much of traditional theology points to insights that should be preserved. The aim is to affirm that awe and mystery are inherently part of human experience, but without ignoring or denying what current scholarship and science seem to substantiate. I have tried to escape magic and mystification but maintain a respect for mystery. That is, I want to reject attempts to limit legitimate knowledge to a narrow version of science.

A primary strategy for accomplishing these goals was to think of God as that which is most sacred—and to think of sacredness as the ultimate form of status. This has allowed me to draw parallels between human-to-human relationships and human-to-Divine relationships. It has the virtue that humans are well acquainted with human relationships and worldly status systems. My claim is that this sociological approach can better help people to grasp the nature of our relationship to the Divine by looking more closely at human-to-human relationships. Of course, there are differences in relationships with other humans and relationships with God.

CONCLUSION

This strategy by itself leaves open what will be treated as sacred. Is this just a matter of personal whim or historical contingency? What is sacralized varies across time and space: a totem animal, a mountain top, a humanly created idol, a tribe, a race, a nation, humanity, nature, free speech, certain kinds of knowledge, or a god. Of course, some people sacralize more than one thing.

The social and ethical problems of contemporary society have not been the focus of this book. Now I want to suggest how the theology that has been outlined bear on some of these concerns. More particularly, I will point out how a theology that does not affirm a transcendent God as the appropriate foundation of ethics is likely to fall short of dealing with the existential and historical problems that confront contemporary humans.

Part of this issue is linked to the difference between what is publicly professed to be sacred and what in fact guides people's actions. In liberal Western democracies such ideals as freedom, choice, equality, and democracy are often mentioned as sacred principles. This is not simply hypocrisy. Nonetheless, the gap between what is professed and what is pursued is often considerable. In most contemporary societies the bottom-line criteria for most politicians are: did "the economy" grow, are incomes up, is unemployment down, is the GDP higher? Similarly, most business CEOs either have to show that the "rate of return" on investment is reasonable or to have very convincing reasons why this is not the appropriate criteria for judging their performance. This is to say, the expansion of wealth has become a "sacred cow" that neither those on the left the right can call into question.

Those who want to qualify or reject the de facto sacralization of the pursuit of wealth tend to sacralize humans. I will mention three examples. One is the human rights movement that has emerged since World War II. While this movement tends to use the language of "rights," in effect it argues that all humans have minimum levels of sacredness that should be recognized and respected. No matter how disreputable or evil an individual or group may be, they should not be tortured or abused, denied due process before the law, nor deprived of at least minimum levels of basic material needs. In practice these rights are often violated, and arguments frequently occur over the boundaries of these rights. Yet, few modern nation-states publicly reject the core concept.[1] A second instance are the efforts within universities to defend the legitimacy and importance of "the humanities"—against the strong tendencies toward seeking "practical" credentials that are seen as more likely to lead to a well-paying job. ("The humanities" were created largely in the nineteenth century to legitimate more secular forms scholarship and to remove them from the supervision of theological faculties.) A third example is the popularity of the term "human flourishing." This is primarily a retranslation of the ancient Greek term *eudaimonia*, which was earlier translated as "happiness." These concepts are largely derived from Aristotelian ethics. In modern thought, these ideas are seen as a rationale for ethical rules that are not dependent on some concept of divine command. As legitimate as these efforts might be, they implicitly deny or play down defining the sacred in more transcendent terms. Humans and their creations are of ultimate value; they should receive the highest status, hence, they should be treated as sacred.

The ecological crisis and seemingly endless wars have made more apparent the depth of human sin: the insensitivity of humans to each other, other species, and the rest of creation. This has made more problematic the assumption that humans are the ultimate sacred referent. While sacralizing humans and developing norms that discourage the mistreatment of one another and the environment are desirable, they are not a sufficient point of reference for dealing with the complexities, contingencies, and mysteries of life. There was a point in time before humans existed. Even with the best imaginable ecological practices, moral sensitivities, and technological developments, human history will come to an end. Of course, we should not seek such an end. Neither should we be in denial.

1. This is why a limited number of "countries," such as North Korea and ISIS (Islamic State of Iraq and Syria) or ISIL (Islamic State of Iraq and the Levant), are viewed as illegitimate rogue regimes. For my more extensive discussion of human rights as a status process, see Milner, *Human Rights as Status Relations*.

CONCLUSION

If so, what is the significance of humans and human history? Is it just a tragic story of the beginning, development, and end of yet another species—and the acknowledgement that the existence of the universe has no significance or meaning? It seems to me that meaning and significance can come only from trust—that is, faith—in something beyond humans; in a God that we partially know, but see only "through a glass darkly." God is one who is near, but whose full otherness is inherently a mystery.

In this book I have affirmed that for me there is a sense of the mysterious presence of God that is my point of reference. I have best experienced this presence in the Christian church—though I make no claim that this is the only way to relate to God. This church was founded on and shaped by our evolving understanding of the life, death, teachings, crucifixion, and resurrection of Jesus. I have experienced this presence in Scripture, preaching, sacraments, music, and interpersonal relationships. I continually fail to live up to my own ideals, the norms of the church, and the teaching of Jesus. Nonetheless, I have felt a sense of forgiveness, acceptance, and a gift of grace. This has enabled me, along with others, to continue the journey. My hope is that it will help others to do likewise.

Appendix

Discussion Questions

USUALLY THE BEST QUESTIONS are the ones that readers raise, but below are some that might be of use to reading groups, adult church classes, or religious studies or theology classes.

Chapter 1: The Problem

1. What is theology?
2. What is a doctrine?
3. Do you agree or disagree with Milner that traditional creeds, prayers, liturgies, and doctrines often call on people to believe the unbelievable?
4. Can you name four key doctrines of your church?
5. Do you usually feel that you understand these doctrines and sincerely affirm them?
6. What in chapter 1 do you most disagree with?

Chapter 2: Religion, Sacredness, and Status

1. What connection does Milner draw between religion, sacredness, and status?
2. Is this useful or confusing or inappropriate?
3. How does status differ from economic or political power?

APPENDIX: DISCUSSION QUESTIONS

Chapter 3: Meaning, Mystery, Magic, Metaphor, and Explanation

1. What gives something meaning?
2. What does mystery mean?
3. What is the difference between explaining and explaining away?
4. How do you think God exercises her/his power?

Chapter 4: Some Classical Doctrines in a New Language

1. Why is the inexpansibility of status a key source of sin?
2. How does the concept of *habitus* help to understand the incarnation?
3. Is the concept of social role a useful way of thinking about the doctrine of the Trinity?
4. Do the sociological concepts clarify these doctrines and make them more meaningful, or do they only add complexity and confusion?

Chapter 5: The Church

1. Why is charismatic leadership always temporary?
2. Have you ever experienced church life as ordinary, mundane, and even petty?
3. In what way are church members equal?
4. Why is it unlikely that there will ever be a completely united church?

APPENDIX: DISCUSSION QUESTIONS

Chapter 6: More Doctrines in a New Language

1. What issue does the doctrine of providence address?
2. What is the difference between general and special revelation?
3. Do you find it helpful to draw a parallel between how people acquire status and the notions of law and grace?
4. If there is a loving God, why is there evil in the world?
5. How useful or offensive to you find it to think of God as a super-CEO?

Chapter 7: Worship

1. What is the difference between worship and magic? Between worship and bargaining?
2. What are the three key processes in worship?
3. Why are notions of sacrifice so common in most religious traditions?
4. What would call into question the legitimacy of a particular worship practice?

Chapter 8: Is There a God?

1. Do you agree that most (and probably all) encompassing views of human existence involve important faith commitments?
2. What is the core belief of the Stoic perspective?
3. What is the difference between optimism and Christian hope?
4. Do you agree or disagree that the expansion of wealth and economic growth have become "sacred cows" that are eroding the sustainability of the planet?

APPENDIX: DISCUSSION QUESTIONS

Chapter 9: Conclusion

1. Do you find the sociological concepts used to interpret theological doctrines and the life of the church helpful, confusing, or alienating?
2. What do you think is treated as sacred in contemporary society?
3. Why are human rights and humanism an inadequate foundation for ethics? For giving a meaning to human existence?

Bibliography

Augustine of Hippo. *Confessions*. Philadelphia: Westminster, 1955.
Baptist Hymnal. Nashville: Southern Baptist Convention, 1975.
Barth, Karl. *The Humanity of God*. Richmond, VA: John Knox, 1960 [1953].
Brauer, Simpon. "The Surprising Predictable Decline of Religion in the United States." *Journal for the Scientific Study of Religion* 57:4 (December 2018) 654–75.
Brueggemann, Walter. *The Prophetic Imagination*. 2nd ed. Minneapolis: Fortress, 2001.
Burley, Mikel. "A Petrification of One's Own Humanity? Nonattachment and Ethics in the Yoga Traditions." *Journal of Religion* 94:2 (April 2014) 204–28.
Buyukgoze-Kavas, Aysenur. "Predicting Career Adaptability from Positive Psychological Traits." *Career Development Quarterly* 64 (June 2016) 114–25.
Calvin, John. *Institutes of the Christian Religion*. Edited by John T. McNeill. 2 vols. Philadelphia: Westminster, 1960 [1559].
Casanova, Jose. "Private and Public Religions." *Social Research* 59:1 (Spring 1992).
Coakley, Sarah. *God, Sexuality, and the Self: An Essay 'On the Trinity'*. Cambridge: Cambridge University Press, 2013.
Cobb, John. *Jesus' Abba: The God Who Has Not Failed*. Minneapolis: Fortress, 2016.
Cone, James H. *The Cross and the Lynching Tree*. Maryknoll, NY: Orbis, 2011.
Cowper, William. "Light Shining Out of Darkness." *Olney Hymns*, 1779.
Douglas, Mary. *Purity and Danger*. London: Routledge and Kegan Paul, 1966.
Dubuisson, Daniel. "Critical Thinking and Comparative Analysis in Religious Studies." *Method and Theory in the Study of Religion* 28:1 (2016) 26–30.
Durkheim, Emile. *The Elementary Forms of Religious Life*. New York: Free Press, 1995 [1912].
European Commission. *Public Opinion*. October 2001. http://ec.europa.eu/commfrontoffice/publicopinion/index.cfm/Chart/getChart/themeKy/18/groupKy/86.

BIBLIOGRAPHY

Feuerbach, Ludwig. "The Contradiction of Faith and Love." In *The Essence of Christianity*, by Ludwig Feuerbach, translated by George Eliot. London: John Chapman, 1854.

Gilkey, Langdon. *On Niebuhr*. Chicago: University of Chicago Press, 2001.

Girard, René, et al. *Violence and the Sacred*. New York: Bloomsbury, 2013 [1972].

Hare, John. "Religion and Morality." *Stanford Encyclopedia of Philosophy*, edited by Edward N. Zalta. Winter 2014 ed. https://plato.stanford.edu/archives/win2014/entries/religion-morality/.

Hartshorne, Charles. *A Natural Theology for Our Time*. La Salle, IL: Open Court, 1965.

Hauerwas, Stanley, and William H. Willimon. *Resident Aliens: Life in the Christian Colony*. Nashville: Abingdon, 1989.

Heim, S. Mark. *Saved from Sacrifice: A Theology of the Cross*. Grand Rapids: Eerdmans, 2006.

Hobson, Theo. *Reinventing Liberal Christianity*. Grand Rapids: Eerdmans, 2013.

Hong, Philip Young P., David R. Hodge, and Sangmi Choi. "Spirituality, Hope, and Self-Sufficiency among Low-Income Job Seekers." *Social Work* 60:2 (April 2015.) 155–64.

Huntington, C. W., Jr. "The Triumph of Narcissism: Theravada Buddhist Meditation in the Market Place." *Journal of the American Academy of Religion* 83:3 (September 2015) 624–48.

Irwin, William. "God Is a Question, Not an Answer." The Stone, *New York Times*, March 26, 2016.

James, William. *The Varieties of Religious Experience*. Gifford Lectures on Natural Religion, 1901–2. New York: Longmans, Green, 1917. http://www.gutenberg.org/files/621/621-h/621-h.html.

Kamitsuka, Margaret D., et al. "Sin and Evil." In *Constructive Theology*, edited by Serene Jones and Paul Lakeland. Minneapolis: Fortress, 2010.

Keller, Catherine. *On the Mystery: Discerning Divinity in Process*. Minneapolis: Fortress, 2008.

Kılınç, Ali Çağatay. "The Relationship between Individual Teacher Academic Optimism and School Climate." *International Online Journal of Educational Sciences* 5:3 (2013) 621–34.

Kivimäki, Mika, et al. "Optimism and Pessimism as Predictors of Change in Health after Death or Onset of Severe Illness in Family." *Health Psychology* 24:4 (2005) 413–42.

Liebman, Robert C., et al. "Exploring the Social Sources of Denominationalism: Schisms in American Protestant Denominations, 1890–1980." *American Sociological Review* 53:3 (June 1988).

Lipka, Michael. "5 Key Findings about the Changing U.S Religious Landscape." Pew Research Center, 2015. http://www.pewresearch.org/fact-tank/2015/05/12/5-key-findings-u-s-religious-landscape/.

Long, Edward LeRoy. *The Nature and Future of Christianity: A Study of Alternative Approaches*. Eugene, OR: Wipf and Stock, 2014.

Mayes, Randolph G. "Theories of Explanation." *Internet Encyclopedia of Philosophy*, edited by James Fieser and Bradley Dowden. https://www.iep.utm.edu/explanat/.

McCoy, Henrika, and Elizabeth A. Bowen. "Hope in the Social Environment: Factors Affecting Future Aspirations and School Self-Efficacy for Youth in Urban Environments." *Child and Adolescent Social Work Journal* 32:2 (April 2015) 131–41.

Milbank, John. *Theology and Social Theory: Beyond Secular Reason*. 2nd ed. Malden, MA: Blackwell, 2006.

Milner, Murray, Jr. *Elites: A General Model*. Malden, MA: Polity, 2015.

———. "Hindu Eschatology and the Indian Caste System: An Example of Structural Reversal." *Journal of Asian Studies* 52:2 (May 1993): 298–319.

———. "Human Rights as Status Relations: A Sociological Approach to Understanding Human Rights." In *Handbook of Human Rights*, edited by Thomas Cushman. London: Routledge, 2012.

———. *Status and Sacredness: A General Theory of Status Relations and an Analysis of Indian Culture*. Oxford: Oxford University Press, 1994.

———. "Status and Sacredness: Worship and Salvation as Forms of Status Transformation." *Journal for the Scientific Study of Religion* 33:2 (June 1994) 99–109.

Moltmann, Jürgen. *The Crucified God: The Cross of Christ as the Foundation and Criticism of Christian Theology*. Translated by John Bowden and R. A. Wilson. Minneapolis: Augsburg Fortress, 1993 [1972].

Mondloch, Michael V., Donald C. Cole, and John W. Frank. "Does How You Do Depend on How You Think You'll Do? A Systematic Review of the Evidence for a Relation between Patients' Recovery Expectations and Health Outcomes." *Canadian Medical Association Journal* 165:2 (July 2001) 174–79.

Ney, Alyssa. "Reductionism." *Internet Encyclopedia of Philosophy*, edited by James Fieser and Bradley Dowden. https://www.iep.utm.edu/red-ism/.

Nouwen, Henri J. M. *Bread for the Journey: A Daybook of Wisdom and Faith*. New York: Harper Collins, 1997.

Office of National Statistics (UK). "Religion in England and Wales 2011." December 2012. https://www.ons.gov.uk/peoplepopulationandcommunity/culturalidentity/religion/articles/religioninenglandandwales2011/2012-12-11.

Otto, Rudolf. *The Idea of the Holy*. 2nd ed. New York: Oxford University Press, 1950.

Patelli, Lorenzo, and Matteo Pedrini. "Is the Optimism in CEO's Letters to Shareholders Sincere? Impression Management versus Communicative Action during the Economic Crisis." *Journal of Business Ethics* 124:1 (2014) 19–34.

Phan, Huy P. "Longitudinal Examination of Optimism, Personal Self-Efficacy and Student Well-Being: A Path Analysis." *Social Psychology of Education* 19:2 (2016) 403–26.

Presbyterian Church (U.S.A.). "Brief Statement of Faith." Adopted 1983. In *The Constitution of the Presbyterian Church (U.S.A.)*, Part 1, *Book of Confessions*, 3011–12. Louisville: Office of the General Assembly, 2016. Online at https://www.presbyterianmission.org/what-we-believe/brief-statement-of-faith/.

Rohr, Richard. "The Christification of the Universe." November 6, 2016. https://cac.org/the-christification-of-the-universe-2016-11-06/.

Schleiermacher, Friedrich. *On Religion: Speeches to Its Cultured Despisers*. Translated by John Oman. New York: Harper and Row, 1958 [1841].

Shortt, Rupert. "A Slave in Your Place." *The Times Literary Supplement*, March 30, 2018.

Smart, Ninian. "Mysticism, History of." *Encyclopedia of Philosophy*. New York: Macmillan, 1967.

Smith, Wilfred Cantwell. *The Meaning and End of Religion*. New York: Macmillan, 1963.

Schlosser, Markus. "Agency." *Stanford Encyclopedia of Philosophy*, edited by Edward N. Zalta. Fall 2015 ed. https://plato.stanford.edu/archives/fall2015/entries/agency/.

Taylor, James E. "The New Atheists." *Internet Encyclopedia of Philosophy*, edited by James Fieser and Bradley Dowden. http://www.iep.utm.edu/n-atheis/.

Tillich, Paul. *Systematic Theology*. 3 vols. Chicago: University of Chicago Press, 1957–65.

Tooley, Michael. "The Problem of Evil." *Stanford Encyclopedia of Philosophy*, edited by Edward N. Zalta. Fall 2015 ed. https://plato.stanford.edu/archives/fall2015/entries/evil/.

Whitehead, Colson. *The Underground Railroad*. New York: Doubleday, 2016.

Ward, Graham. *The Postmodern God: A Theological Reader*. Malden, MA: Blackwell, 1990. See the Introduction, xv–xlvii.

Williams, Rowan. *Tokens of Trust: An Introduction of Christian Belief*. Louisville: Westminster John Knox, 2007.

Willimon, William H. "The Trinity: God's Unprofessional Nearness." Delivered at Duke University Chapel, Trinity Sunday, June 10, 1990. https://repository.duke.edu/download/duke:317342.

Wood, Charles M. "Providence." Ch. 5 in *The Oxford Handbook of Systematic Theology*, edited by John Webster, Kathryn Tanner, and Iain Torrance, 91–104. Oxford: Oxford University Press, 2007.

Index

atheism, 101
alliances, 25–27, 66
   social, 25–27
   with the divine, 66
association, 12, 16, 51, 69–71, 78,
   85–90, 92
   And intimacy, 16

Barth, Karl, 8, 67, 75
belief, xi, 4–5, 39, 44, 60, 89, 95
boundaries, 6, 11, 16, 58, 108
   and schisms , 6
Bourdieu, Pierre, 40
Brueggemann, Walter, 74
Brunner, Emil, 8
Bultmann, Rudolf, 39

charisma, 30, 42, 52, 54
   routinization of, 54
church, xi-xii, 1–3, 14, 50–62, 69,
   75, 82, 88, 91–92, 100, 103,
   109
   and the world, 60–62
   as a "turnoff", 51–52
   as sinners, 57
   as a 12-step group, 71
   centrality of Jesus, 52–53
   decline, xii, 9
   handling disagreements, 7
   hypocrisy, 51
   members, not fans but players,
      56–57

   why join, 54–56
   ways of relating to the world, 61
Christ, 23, 38–39, 42–44, 52, 55,
   57–58, 67–68, 70, 72–73, 76,
   78, 88, 94, 105
Coakley, Sarah, 4, 8
Cobb, John, 21
Cone, James, 74
confessions of faith, 92–93
conformity, 15, 69, 71, 78, 90
consumer capitalism, 99–100
Cowper, William, 66
creeds, 8–9, 92
crucifixion, 38, 45, 53, 62, 74–75,
   82, 100, 109

Darwin, Charles, 22
decline of, 9, 83
   mainline churches, 9
   religion, 83
disagreements, 7, 54
doctrine, xi-xii, 2–7, 42, 52, 65, 67,
   69, 72–76, 78, 81–82, 90,
   106
   informational and evaluative,
      xi-xii
   unbelievable, 5
doubt, 59, 95–96
Durkheim, Emile, 12, 65, 102–103

eating, 16, 52, 88
ecological crisis, 108

INDEX

economic growth and wealth, 9, 100, 107
education, 2, 7, 10, 62
elaboration of norms, 15
eschatology, 68, 76, 78
evil, 1, 24, 27, 33–35, 38, 46, 64, 68, 73, 78–82, 93, 107
   problem of, 38, 46, 64, 78–79
   and tragedy, 78–79
explanation, 22, 103

faith responses, 96, 98, 100
   stoicism, 96–97, 99, 104
   epicureanism, 96, 98–99, 104
   theism, 83, 96, 99–101, 104
faith, 57, 62, 69, 92–102, 109
Feuerbach, Ludwig, 27, 102

Gilkey, Langdon, 19
God, 5, 10, 21, 28–31, 38–39, 41–42, 46, 48, 53, 57–58, 60, 63–71, 102–107, 109
   as the most sacred, 106
   different ways of experiencing, 48, 53
   names for, 38
   limits her/his power, 28–29, 80–82
   as the creation of humans, 102–105
grace, 59–60, 68–71, 75, 78, 84, 87, 92, 94, 109
groups, realness of, 48

Hartshorne, Charles, 8, 83
Heim, Mark, 75
hope, 25, 42, 53, 61, 76, 101
   versus optimism, 100–101
humility, 20, 23, 26, 66, 96

Irwin, William, 95

James, William, 23

justice, 2, 5, 54–55, 58, 62, 72, 75, 78, 94, 99
incarnation, 38, 40–43, 65, 75, 82
intimacy, 16, 36, 71, 73, 82, 84, 88–90, 94
   sex and eating, 16, 88
   and status, 71, 84
Jesus, 20–21, 24, 38–44, 52–53, 55–60, 62, 67–78, 88, 93–94, 105, 109

Kamitsuka, Margaret D, 33
Keller, Catherine, 42

language, 1–4, 40, 51, 65, 86–87, 89
law and grace, 69, 78
Lord's prayer, 92–93
Luther, Martin, 69

magic, 5, 17, 24, 65, 78, 84, 91, 104, 106
meaning, 17–19, 37, 71, 73, 99, 104, 109
meditation, 4, 28, 55–56, 64–65, 67, 81, 84–85, 90, 98
megachurches, 9, 91
Merton, Thomas, 95
metalanguage, 3
metaphor, 17, 20–21, 24, 43, 48, 71, 75, 77, 81, 82, 106
Moltmann, Jurgen, 8, 46–47
monasticism, 90
Morris, Colin, 45
mystery, 5, 17, 19, 24, 64, 66, 78, 82, 106, 109

norms, 15, 31, 69, 85–86, 103, 108–109

optimism, 100–101
Orwell, George, 57
otherness, of God, 5, 54, 103, 109

pluralism, 14, 50, 58–59

INDEX

power, 13, 15, 21, 28–31, 58, 87
  nature of God's, 21, 28
  forms of, 13, 21, 28, 29, 55
  God's self-imposed limits, 80
  prayer, 31, 64, 67, 70, 72, 81, 89–94
  problem, with creeds and theology, 92
profane, 11–12, 28, 54, 60–62, 64, 84–85, 92
providence, 64–66, 81, 100
putdowns, 14

resurrection, 30, 42, 53, 55, 65, 67, 94, 105, 109
Reuther, Rosemary Radford, 8
revelation, 42, 66–68, 100
ritual, 30, 74, 84–85, 103
Rohr, Richard, 42

sacrifice, 72–75, 78, 80, 89
sacredness, 4, 10–13, 16, 24, 31, 41, 70, 91, 106–107
  and the profane, 12, 54, 64, 84
  special characteristics of, 24–25
salvation, 39, 55, 68–71, 76–79, 83
Schleiermacher, Fredrich, 27
sex, 16, 88
sin, 1, 28, 32, 33–38, 40, 68–69, 73, 75, 79–80, 86, 89, 100, 108
Spirit, Holy, 1, 30, 43–46, 49, 58–59, 65, 86, 88, 93
St. Augustine of Hippo, 35, 40, 43, 69, 72
St Thomas Aquinas, 3
status, 3–4, 12–16, 24, 28–32, 35–36, 65–66, 69, 73, 84–86, 100, 108
  and association, 16, 78, 86
  and conformity, 15, 69, 78, 90
  as sacredness, 4, 12–13
  definition of status, 3, 13

inexpansibility, 13–14, 26
inalienability, 14, 26, 36
theory of status relations, 12
versus economic and political power, 13
status systems, 3–4, 8, 12, 35, 58, 88, 106

theologians, xi, 3–5 , 8, 27, 35, 39, 42, 47, 67, 74–75, 82
theology, 3–5, 7–8, 10, 22–24, 30, 40, 76, 78, 80, 82, 104, 107
  as paradoxical, 5
  definition of, 4
  liberation theology, 10
  feminist theology, 10
  for whom, 8–10
  positive and negative, 5
  process theology, 3, 30, 80
  sociological theology, 4
Tillich, Paul, 3, 8, 17, 39, 63
trinity, 43–45, 47–50, 53, 67, 80
trust, 9, 34, 109

Union Theological Seminary, 8

Volf, Miroslav, 47

Whithead, Alfred North, 3
worship, 5, 26, 31, 47, 56, 60, 65–67, 70, 79, 82, 84–94, 103
  and sacrifice, 89
  preparation and confession, 85–86
  praise of the deity, 86–87
  intimacy with the deity, 88–89
  styles of, 91–92
  versus bargaining, 84
  and sacrifice, prayer, and preaching, 89–90
  and mysticism, 89–90

www.ingramcontent.com/pod-product-compliance
Lightning Source LLC
Chambersburg PA
CBHW050834160426
43192CB00010B/2026